Joseph Barber Lightfoot

Cambridge sermons

Joseph Barber Lightfoot

Cambridge sermons

ISBN/EAN: 9783337085834

Printed in Europe, USA, Canada, Australia, Japan

Cover: Foto ©Andreas Hilbeck / pixelio.de

More available books at **www.hansebooks.com**

CAMBRIDGE SERMONS

BY THE LATE

JOSEPH BARBER LIGHTFOOT, D.D., D.C.L., LL.D.,
LORD BISHOP OF DURHAM

PUBLISHED BY THE TRUSTEES OF THE LIGHTFOOT FUND

London
MACMILLAN AND CO.
AND NEW YORK
1890

All Rights reserved

EXTRACT FROM THE LAST WILL AND TESTAMENT OF THE LATE JOSEPH BARBER LIGHTFOOT, LORD BISHOP OF DURHAM.

"I bequeath all my personal Estate not herein-
"before otherwise disposed of unto [my Executors]
"upon trust to pay and transfer the same unto the
"Trustees appointed by me under and by virtue of a
"certain Indenture of Settlement creating a Trust to
"be known by the name of 'The Lightfoot Fund for
"the Diocese of Durham' and bearing even date
"herewith but executed by me immediately before
"this my Will to be administered and dealt with by
"them upon the trusts for the purposes and in the
"manner prescribed by such Indenture of Settle-
"ment."

EXTRACT FROM THE INDENTURE OF SETTLEMENT OF 'THE LIGHTFOOT FUND FOR THE DIOCESE OF DURHAM.'

"WHEREAS the Bishop is the Author of and is
"absolutely entitled to the Copyright in the several
"Works mentioned in the Schedule hereto, and for the

vi   *Extract from Bishop Lightfoot's Will.*

"purposes of these presents he has assigned or intends
"forthwith to assign the Copyright in all the said
"Works to the Trustees. Now the Bishop doth
"hereby declare and it is hereby agreed as follows :—

"The Trustees (which term shall hereinafter be
"taken to include the Trustees for the time being of
"these presents) shall stand possessed of the said
"Works and of the Copyright therein respectively
"upon the trusts following (that is to say) upon trust
"to receive all moneys to arise from sales or otherwise
"from the said Works, and at their discretion from
"time to time to bring out new editions of the same
"Works or any of them, or to sell the copyright in
"the same or any of them, or otherwise to deal with
"the same respectively, it being the intention of
"these presents that the Trustees shall have and
"may exercise all such rights and powers in respect
"of the said Works and the copyright therein re-
"spectively, as they could or might have or exercise
"in relation thereto if they were the absolute bene-
"ficial owners thereof....

"The Trustees shall from time to time, at such
"discretion as aforesaid, pay and apply the income
"of the Trust funds for or towards the erecting,
"rebuilding, repairing, purchasing, endowing, sup-
"porting, or providing for any Churches, Chapels,
"Schools, Parsonages, and Stipends for Clergy, and

"other Spiritual Agents in connection with the
"Church of England and within the Diocese of
"Durham, and also for or towards such other pur-
"poses in connection with the said Church of
"England, and within the said Diocese, as the
"Trustees may in their absolute discretion think fit,
"provided always that any payment for erecting any
"building, or in relation to any other works in con-
"nection with real estate, shall be exercised with due
"regard to the Law of Mortmain; it being declared
"that nothing herein shall be construed as intended
"to authorise any act contrary to any Statute or
"other Law....

"In case the Bishop shall at any time assign to
"the Trustees any Works hereafter to be written or
"published by him, or any Copyrights, or any other
"property, such transfer shall be held to be made for
"the purposes of this Trust, and all the provisions
"of this Deed shall apply to such property, subject
"nevertheless to any direction concerning the same
"which the Bishop may make in writing at the time
"of such transfer, and in case the Bishop shall at any
"time pay any money, or transfer any security, stock,
"or other like property to the Trustees, the same
"shall in like manner be held for the purposes of this
"Trust, subject to any such contemporaneous direc-
"tion as aforesaid, and any security, stock or pro-

"perty so transferred, being of a nature which can
"lawfully be held by the Trustees for the purposes
"of these presents, may be retained by the Trustees,
"although the same may not be one of the securities
"hereinafter authorised.

"The Bishop of Durham and the Archdeacons of
"Durham and Auckland for the time being shall be
"*ex-officio* Trustees, and accordingly the Bishop and
"Archdeacons, parties hereto, and the succeeding
"Bishops and Archdeacons, shall cease to be Trus-
"tees on ceasing to hold their respective offices, and
"the number of the other Trustees may be increased,
"and the power of appointing Trustees in the place
"of Trustees other than Official Trustees, and of
"appointing extra Trustees, shall be exercised by
"Deed by the Trustees for the time being, provided
"always that the number shall not at any time be
"less than five.

"The Trust premises shall be known by the name
"of 'The Lightfoot Fund for the Diocese of Durham.'"

CONTENTS.

TRINITY COLLEGE CHAPEL SERMONS.

PAGE

I. ESAU.

And when Esau heard the words of his father, he cried with a great and exceeding bitter cry, and said unto his father, Bless me, even me also, O my father.
GENESIS xxvii. 34. . 3

II. THE CONQUEROR FROM EDOM.

Who is this that cometh from Edom, with dyed garments from Bozrah?
ISAIAH lxiii. 1. . 19

III. PURITY OF HEART.

Blessed are the pure in heart: for they shall see God.
S. MATTHEW v. 8. . 34

IV. TWO SOWINGS AND TWO HARVESTS.

Be not deceived; God is not mocked: for whatsoever a man soweth, that shall he also reap. For he that soweth to his flesh shall of the flesh reap corruption; but he that soweth to the Spirit shall of the Spirit reap life everlasting.
GALATIANS vi. 7, 8. . 48

CONTENTS.

PAGE

V. EXCEPT IT DIE.

That which thou sowest is not quickened, except it die.
1 CORINTHIANS xv. 36. . 63

VI. THE ONE GOD AND THE GODS MANY.

Though there be that are called gods, whether in heaven or in earth, (as there be gods many, and lords many), but to us there is but one God, the Father, of Whom are all things, and we for (unto) Him.
1 CORINTHIANS viii. 5. . 80

VII. THE MIRROR OF GOD'S GLORY.

We all with open face beholding as in a glass the glory of the Lord, are changed into the same image from glory to glory.
2 CORINTHIANS iii. 18. . 96

VIII. WHAT ADVANTAGETH IT?

If after the manner of men I have fought with beasts at Ephesus, what advantageth it me? If the dead rise not, let us eat and drink, for to-morrow we die.
1 CORINTHIANS xv. 32. . 109

UNIVERSITY SERMONS.

                                                            PAGE

I. SHEW US THE FATHER.

Philip saith unto Him, Lord, shew us the Father, and it sufficeth us. Jesus saith unto him, Have I been so long time with you, and yet hast thou not known Me, Philip? He that hath seen Me, hath seen the Father; and how sayest thou then, Shew us the Father?

                                   S. JOHN xiv. 8, 9. . 129

II. THE SWORD OF THE WORD.

The word of God is quick, and powerful, and sharper than any two-edged sword, piercing even to the dividing asunder of soul and spirit, and of the joints and marrow, and is a discerner of the thoughts and intents of the heart. Neither is there any creature that is not manifest in His sight: but all things are naked and opened to the eyes of Him with Whom we have to do.

                                   HEBREWS iv. 12, 13. . 150

III. THE HEAD AND THE BODY.

That we may grow up into Him in all things, Which is the head, even Christ; from Whom the whole body fitly joined together and compacted by that which every joint supplieth, according to the effectual working in the measure of every part, maketh increase of the body unto the edifying of itself in love.

                                  EPHESIANS iv. 15, 16. . 172

IV. THE WRATH OF THE LAMB.

The wrath of the Lamb.

                                   REVELATION vi. 16. . 193

CONTENTS.

PAGE

V. THE REVEALER OF THE HEART.
The saying of the woman, which testified, He told me all that ever I did.
S. JOHN iv. 39. . 212

VI. THE MEANNESS AND THE GREATNESS OF MAN.
What is man, that Thou art mindful of him; and the son of man, that Thou visitest him?
PSALM viii. 4. . 229

VII. OFFENCES.
It must needs be that offences come; but woe to that man by whom the offence cometh!
S. MATTHEW xviii. 7. . 248

VIII. FOLLY AND WEAKNESS TRIUMPHANT.
The foolishness of God is wiser than men; and the weakness of God is stronger than men.
1 CORINTHIANS i. 25. . 265

IX. BOUGHT WITH A PRICE.
Ye are bought with a price.
1 CORINTHIANS vi. 20. . 283

X. BETHEL.
Surely the Lord is in this place; and I knew it not.
GENESIS xxviii. 16. . 300

XI. TRUE AMBITION.
I can do all things through Christ which strengtheneth me.
PHILIPPIANS iv. 13. . 317

PREACHED IN

TRINITY COLLEGE CHAPEL,

1861—1875.

C. S.

I.

ESAU.

And when Esau heard the words of his father, he cried with a great and exceeding bitter cry, and said unto his father, Bless me, even me also, O my father.

GENESIS xxvii. 34.

.Trinity College Chapel, 24th Sunday after Trinity, 1861.

IT is to be feared that even those who are most ready to confess that all Holy Scripture was written for our learning, do yet practically derive very little instruction from large portions of the Old Testament History. There are certain broad features indeed which we can scarcely mistake. When the flagrant sinner is struck down by divine vengeance in the midst of his crimes, or when blessings are showered on the faithful servant of God, the lesson is too plain to escape us. The history of David or of Ahab cannot be misread. But there are other parts of Holy Scripture which appear to us very perplexing and unintelligible, which we are disposed perhaps to give up in despair. We cannot understand for instance why in certain cases grave sins are dealt with so lightly, or slight offences visited with so heavy a punishment. We feel that our measure of right and wrong would have been very different; that we should have established another law of retribution. There are many reasons for this. It arises in part no doubt because we are judging of past ages by the conventional standard of good and evil in our own, and are therefore unwilling to view some of the more current and respectable sins in their true light. But it is still more due to the circumstance, that the point which decides the true character of the action frequently does not lie on the surface of the narrative, and that it requires more pains perhaps than we are disposed to give, in order to appreciate its moral significance. And yet it is just those lessons requiring the most study to master which are the most valuable, when once learnt. For they not only give us the broad features of God's dealings with His creatures. They bring out the finer lines in the portraiture of good and evil. They develope the faint shadows of the picture. They discriminate between the real and the seeming. And thus they bring home to us our true position in the sight of God. They pluck off the mask, which we have worn to ourselves as well as to others. They penetrate the inmost depths of our spirit. And thus 'the word of God is' indeed 'quick, and powerful, and sharper than any two-edged sword,' a very 'discerner of the thoughts and intents of the heart.'

And it happens very frequently in such cases—where the lesson conveyed does not appear at once on the face of the narrative, and where consequently there is a danger of our passing it over in a careless reading—that our attention is arrested by some casual but pointed allusion to it in the writings of an Apostle or Evangelist, or in the words of our Blessed Lord Himself. And thus the light of the New Testament is shed upon the Old. The narrative assumes a new aspect. We at length recognise its importance. We are led to study it afresh, and each time we read it we are more fully impressed with the depth of the lesson it conveys.

The instances of Balaam and of Esau both illustrate the truth of what I have been saying. They are in many respects parallel. The difficulty is much the same in either case. We are at a loss to account for the extreme severity, as we are disposed to regard it, with which the offender is treated in the sacred narrative. Both alike are referred to in the New Testament. 'The way of Balaam the son of Bosor' is a by-word for disobedience and ungodliness. The 'profane' Esau, 'who for one morsel of meat sold his birthright', is the very picture and type of the hopelessly and irrevocably fallen.

Yet this is certainly not the estimate we should have formed by ourselves. Our first impression of Balaam is of one, who—if he fell short of the highest perfection, if his duty to God was not all in all to him—yet at all events cannot be said to have gone very far wrong. We read of his consulting God in all he does. We find him acting as God commands him to act. We marvel at his subsequent history, and we are perplexed at the language which Scripture holds regarding him. So again with Esau. We have a sort of feeling that he too, like Balaam, is somewhat hardly dealt with. We are not sure that we should have given the preference to his brother Jacob—nay, we more than suspect that we should have reversed the judgment: that, instead of depriving him of the blessing, we should even have restored him the birthright. We have a lurking regard for his rough, impetuous, simple character, for his undesigning and generous spirit. The treachery which is practised upon him, and the success which attends his brother's plots, enlist our sympathies in his favour. It is only when we have examined the narratives more closely, giving them more thought and trying to divest ourselves of our prejudices, that we see their history in its true light. Then at length we acknowledge the justice of God's rebuke of Balaam; and we cease to marvel at his fall, because we can now see that, when he acted aright, he acted from fear and not from love. Then at length we discover the superiority of Jacob; and we wonder no more that Esau was deprived of the blessing and rejected as a profane person : for we see that Jacob—though amidst many imperfections, despite many grievous sins—did place his reliance on God; did look to Him, as the Giver of all good things; did live for more than the passing moment. In short Jacob was spiritually minded; while Esau—with much in him to like, and something to admire—was careless and indifferent to all higher things, influenced only by passing impulses and momentary impressions, without foresight, without reflection, the type of that hopeless class of men, whose maxim is, 'Let us eat and drink, for to-morrow we die.'

To this latter narrative, the history of Esau, I will ask your attention for a few moments this morning. I know of no sadder story. I can imagine none. If the character of Esau had been less attractive, his fall would have excited less pity. If his prospects had not been so brilliant, his fate would have been less terrible. But it is the combination of these two circumstances in the narrative—the ruin of a character which we are disposed to admire, and the unspeakable value of the birthright and the blessing which he recklessly threw away—that gives the interest to the story, and rivets our attention to the lesson which it contains. The destruction of so many bright hopes, the dissipation of so many glorious visions, the hopeless and irrevocable ruin of one so simple and honest and open-hearted—what can be more touching than this? And hence it is that we seem to hear ringing sharply above the most piercing shrieks of pain, and the loudest wailings of grief, that one exceeding bitter cry, uttered in the agony of despair, 'Bless me, even me also, O my father.'

And perhaps it may be that the narrative comes home with peculiar force to ourselves, that we are conscious of some crisis in our own lives, or recall some incident in the career of others whom we have known and loved, which reminds us only too painfully of the fate of Esau, and gives point to the lesson. Is it so with any of us? May it not be so in some degree or other with most or all of us? Or is it a mere form that we bewail our manifold sins and wickednesses; that we confess the remembrance of them to be grievous unto us, the burden intolerable? Have we not each our special temptation, our besetting sin? And it may be that at one time or other this has culminated in some act, more heinous than we had supposed possible—some breach of the law of love, or of truth, or of purity, according to our special temptation—one act which has seemed to shut us out from the presence of God, and to leave us to darkness and despair. And then at length we have learnt in our bitter anguish to measure the exceeding great value of that heavenly birthright, which as sons of God we have inherited only to spurn and to set at naught, and—in remorse, if not in penitence—have striven by the importunity of our cries to arrest the blessing, ere it has passed away from us for ever.

I need scarcely dwell on the character of Esau, as it is painted in the sacred narrative. Making allowance for the rude habits of the patriarchal age, he is not essentially different in character from a very large number among ourselves. He has just the same virtues, and just the same faults. He is the father's favourite son. He is born to great hopes. He has brilliant prospects before him. His career is in his own hands. His lot may well be envied by others. But all is thrown away upon him. He is reckless of his opportunities. He is insensible to his blessings. He loses everything by one desperate act of folly. He finds out too late the value of what he has lost. He would give anything to recover it, when recovering it is hopeless. And yet his character is far from utterly vicious. Of such a man we might say, that he is no one's enemy but his own. If his bad passions are strong, his impulses for good are strong also. If he is reckless and undisciplined, he is simple and honest and open-hearted. He is in short not so very much worse—perhaps not at all worse—than a great number, who are admired and loved among ourselves, and whose manifest faults are forgiven for the sake of many rough virtues and generous affections.

Nor do I think that the guilt of Esau will seem so much deeper in comparison with that which we may incur, when we consider the nature of the privilege which he despised, of the blessing which he threw away. True it is that the promise which pertained to Esau—the promise given to Abraham and renewed to Isaac—was something more than the possession of lands and flocks and houses; that his birthright implied more than mere rank or wealth or earthly power. He knew that by virtue of his birthright he was destined to be the father of the chosen seed; that in him all the families of the earth should be blessed; that from his race as concerning the flesh Christ was to come, the Redeemer of the whole world. This he knew, or might have known. This inheritance he bartered for a morsel of meat. For this he is condemned and branded as a profane person.

It was no common offence then of which Esau was guilty. It was perhaps as great an offence as in his position he could have committed. Yet it is not greater than that which we shall commit, if like him we despise our birthright. For have we not an inheritance more precious still—we who are heirs of God and joint-heirs with Christ—a name more glorious than his, for it is a name better than of sons and of daughters? If he might have been the father of Messiah's race, how much greater is our privilege, to whom is accorded a far more intimate, because a spiritual, relationship? 'Whosoever shall do the will of My Father Which is in heaven, the same is My brother and sister and mother.' Are we tempted for some worldly consideration, for some momentary advantage, for wealth or popularity or fame or ease or pleasure, to barter away this brilliant inheritance? Is not the price we give as ruinous, the exchange we get as worthless, as it was with Esau?

There are two circumstances however in the story of Esau, which it may be well to dwell on more at length: for from these we may derive the most valuable lesson. Yet at first sight they only perplex us. They seem not only to palliate the guilt, but almost to obliterate the offence. They lead us to look upon him as the victim rather than the culprit, as sinned against rather than sinning. The first of these is the circumstance that he is surprised into selling his birthright. It is a momentary, unpremeditated act; he falls into a snare laid for him; we feel disposed therefore not to judge him too harshly: we cannot regard his offence as very heinous. In the second place, though the loss of the birthright was certainly his own act, whatever excuse we may make for it, yet he was deprived of the blessing by no fault of his. By no reasonable foresight could he have prevented it. He made some efforts at least to obtain that blessing. He did not throw it away. He was robbed of it. Surely this can not be laid to his charge. Of this at least he is innocent.

In considering the first of these points, let us ask ourselves what is meant by being surprised into such and such a sinful act—what leads to it, what state of mind it supposes, how it comes about? In a certain sense indeed Esau *is* surprised into selling his birthright. He returns from the field hungry and faint. He asks for food. His brother will not give it him except at the price of his birthright. He yields. 'Behold,' he says, 'I am at the point to die: and what profit shall this birthright do to me?' But is this yielding an isolated act? Does it not show a defective character? Does it not betoken a certain spiritual depravity, a low, worldly view of his position? He 'despised his birthright,' we are told, and therefore he is branded as 'a profane person.'

For indeed surprise would be utterly powerless,

unless the character were previously undermined. And so it is no excuse for a sinful act; it is scarcely in any degree a palliation. It is rather a revelation of secret depravity in a man, hidden successfully from his neighbours, ignored by, but not unknown to, himself. After the flagrant deed is committed, others may be at a loss to account for it. It is unexplained to them by anything in his previous career. But to himself it is clear enough. To him it is not an isolated act, but one link in a long chain of evil. He has been aware all along that he was sinking into sin. He has thrust away the troublesome thought, but he has been aware of it. He has taken no measure, it may be, of the growth of his guilt. It has ripened into grievous sin unnoticed. In no other sense can it have been a surprise to him. For all the while the seed was there, and had taken root, and the noxious plant was growing; and he knew it, and he hid it from others, and he would not confess it perhaps even to himself.

Is it an act of sensuality into which he has been betrayed? One act perhaps, which has poisoned the fountains of his spiritual life, which has bound his outward existence with heavy chains which he cannot shake off. The temptation took him unawares, we say. He was startled into sin. But is this the whole account of the matter? Is it natural, is it reasonable, that this should be so? Who shall dare to trace the secret history of that man's soul, to lay open the hidden springs of his guilt? Who shall venture to say what forbidden thoughts he has admitted, perhaps welcomed, how recklessly he has lingered on the border line of good and evil, how longingly he has hovered about the accursed thing, before he dared to touch it?

Or again, is it a palpable breach of truth or honesty? He has committed some act of fraud or treachery, which has destroyed his good name for ever. How came this to pass? Were there no antecedents in his career which led naturally to that result? Had he not contracted a habit, for instance, of saying less or more than he meant, of expressing an enthusiasm or an interest which he did not feel, of paring down the truth to fit it into some conventional mould, of suppressing a little here or exaggerating a little there? Or if he fell, not from moral cowardice or from the desire to please, but from greed of gain, were there not here also insidious influences at work? There are many cases, where the question of right is doubtful. These he has decided in his own favour. There are others, where, if he investigated, he might find that he was defrauding his neighbour. These he will not enquire into. He will not be dishonest knowingly, but he will take no pains to find whether he is so or not. These are the beginnings of his guilt. By these a fraudulent habit is created. By degrees he goes on from bad to worse. He avails himself of his superior cunning; he defrauds his neighbour in little things where he is sure of escaping observation. By this time he has ceased to respect honesty as a thing to be prized in itself. To him it is so much capital to trade upon—and for this purpose the semblance is as good as the reality. Hitherto he has preserved his reputation before the world. But at length he is surprised, as we say, into some flagrant act of dishonesty. Society lays him under a ban. His character is irrecoverably lost.

And so it was with Esau. It was not that one act of selling his birthright which constituted his guilt. That was but the revelation of his true character, the summing up, as it were, of his depravity.

But fearful as is the lesson which this incident suggests, it is not half so fearful as that which we derive from his subsequent fate. He bartered away his birthright, but how was it with the blessing? It was by no act of his own that he lost this. There is nothing in the narrative which leads us to such a supposition. There was no unholy traffic here, no profane contempt here. He did not drive the blessing away. It went in spite of him. The key to this difficulty is found in the allusion in the Epistle to the

Hebrews. The loss of the blessing is there represented as the inevitable consequence of the sale of his birthright. 'Ye know that afterwards, when he would have inherited the blessing, he was rejected.' His fate up to a certain point was in his own hands. After that it was placed beyond his reach. So it was with Esau, and so it is always with the downward course of guilt. We may wade for a time amidst the shallows of sin, feeling our footing and heedless of danger. A single step more places us at the mercy of the waves, and we are swept away into the ocean of ruin. When we read of God's hardening the sinner's heart, we are perhaps startled at the phrase, yet there is no doubt that it represents a fearful moral truth. The sinner after a time ceases to be his own master. He has coiled a chain about him, which binds him hand and foot. He is dragged helplessly down. There is no more terrible passage in classical literature than that in which the Roman poet describes the guilty man trembling in his secret soul, as he sees himself falling, falling headlong, unheeded and unsuspected by those nearest to him. With a true moral insight he regards this state as the just retribution of offended heaven—the heaviest punishment which can be inflicted on the most heinous guilt. Such indeed it is. Translating it into the language of Scripture we should say, that God has hardened such a man's heart. Surely we need not call to our aid the terrors of an unseen world— however true those terrors may be—to deter us from the path of guilt. The thought that our hearts also may be hardened, that we too may shut ourselves out from the presence of God, should be sufficient to check us in our downward career.

And even supposing this deadness should not pervade our whole spiritual being, may not the yielding to our special temptation, the indulgence in our favourite sin, stiffen and paralyse some limb or other of our moral frame? Do we not every now and then see an instance of this? We are brought in contact with some one, who, thoroughly conscientious in most things, keenly sensitive on many points of duty, is yet hardened in some one point of his moral constitution, seems dead to some moral virtue. Yet such cases are exceptional. It is the tendency of this paralysis to spread. It seizes on one limb first, but presently it extends to all. The moral frame, like the bodily, is compacted and knit together in a marvellous way. There is a wonderful sympathy between limb and limb. 'Whether one member suffer, all the members suffer with it; or one member be honoured, all the members rejoice with it.'

In what I have said, I have been speaking the language of warning, and not the language of despair.

Despair is no word of the Christian's vocabulary. So long as there is any heavenward aspiration, any loathing of sin, any yearning after better things, however slight, however feeble, there is still hope. Cherish these higher feelings. Quench not the Spirit, though it flicker faintly and lowly. From these few sparks a bright flame may be kindled, which shall cheer your heart, and throw a light upon your path, and guide you home to your heavenly rest.

II.

THE CONQUEROR FROM EDOM.

Who is this that cometh from Edom, with dyed garments from Bozrah?

ISAIAH lxiii. 1.

Trinity College Chapel, 3rd Sunday in Lent, 1868.

THE feud between Edom and Israel had been long and bitter. The descendants of the brothers Jacob and Esau, living as near neighbours, viewed each other with no brotherly or neighbourly eye. The conflict began at a very early date. When the Israelites, set free from Egypt and traversing the desert, asked permission to pass through the territory of the Edomites, the request was churlishly refused. In vain did they plead that they would do no injury to person or property; that they would avoid fields and vineyards and keep to the highway; that they would even pay for the water which they might drink. 'Edom refused to give Israel passage through his border; wherefore Israel turned away from him.'

This rude and unbrotherly repulse was neither forgotten nor forgiven. Established in the land of promise, the Israelites appear very frequently at war, very rarely in alliance, with the Edomites. 'Who will lead me into the strong city? Who will bring me into Edom? Wilt not Thou, O God, go forth with our hosts?' This is the climax of the Psalmist's prayer—repeated in two different psalms—when Israel is engaged in a fierce contest with this brother tribe.

And this hereditary feud continued to the latest days of Israel, now smouldering treacherously and now bursting out into flames—a feud far worse than the generous antagonism of declared enemies. For there is always a wretched meanness, a low malice, an exaggeration of bitterness—arising out of the false position—in the quarrels of those, whom God and nature have intended to be friends. It is when two peoples of the same race and language go to war, when a nation is divided against itself by civil dissensions, when members of one family fall out, that the worst passions of man's nature have full play.

But it was in the day of Israel's deepest sorrow, that Edom's iniquity reached its climax. When their sharpest pang overtook the Israelites, when their enemies beleaguered them, when their palaces were rifled and their walls thrown down, when their sons and their daughters were swept away into captivity, some change might have been looked for in the attitude of the Edomites. Surely now the moment was come, when past injuries and long-embittered feuds should be forgotten, when the true fraternal love should well up in their hearts, when brother once more should run to meet brother, and embrace him and fall on his neck and kiss him. But, unlike his forefather, Edom had now no tenderness, no compassion for Israel's sorrow. With a fiendish glee he looked on at the catastrophe. The great Babylonian conqueror was delivering him from a dangerous enemy, a troublesome neighbour—a troublesome brother, it might be said, but what cared he for this? Who made him his brother's keeper? It was this heartless display of cruel satisfaction, which called forth the bitter cry for vengeance from the exiles on the banks of the Euphrates, interrupting so strangely the plaintive elegy of the mourners: 'Remember the children of Edom, O Lord, in the day of Jerusalem; how they said, Down with it, down with it, even to the ground.'

Then it was, in the hour of Israel's humiliation, that Edom 'stood on the other side;' that 'in the day that the stranger carried away captive Israel's forces and foreigners entered into his gates,' Edom was 'even as one of them;' that 'in the day of their destruction' Edom 'rejoiced over the children of Judah,' and 'in the day of distress spake proudly;' that Edom 'stood in the cross-way to cut off them that did escape.'

It was for this, that the prophet Obadiah predicted a terrible vengeance on this unfeeling race. 'The day of the Lord is near upon all the heathen: as thou hast done, it shall be done unto thee: thy reward shall return upon thine own head.' 'The house of Jacob shall be a fire, and the house of Joseph a flame, and the house of Esau for stubble, and they shall kindle in them, and devour them.' It was for this that the two great prophets of the fall and captivity, the one an exile on the banks of the Chebar, the other lingering still among the ruins of the holy city, Ezekiel and Jeremiah, the strophe and antistrophe of the same tragedy, 'deep answering deep' (as it has been said) 'across the Assyrian desert,' join in denouncing God's judgment on the offending Edom.

And in this chorus of inspired utterances, early and late, the voice of the Evangelic prophet is not silent. Raising his eyes, he sees approaching from the south-eastern frontier, from the direction of Edom, and of Bozrah the capital of Edom, a sublime form, as of some mighty hero, advancing with majestic step, and clad in the scarlet robes of a victorious captain.

Awed at the sight, he asks, 'Who is this that cometh from Edom, with dyed garments from Bozrah? This that is glorious in His apparel, travelling in the greatness of His strength?' A voice replies, 'I am He that speaketh in righteousness, mighty to save.' It is the just and upright judge, the terrible avenger, the powerful and saving ally, the triumphant king, the Lord Jehovah Himself. As the sublime form approaches, the prophet sees that His scarlet robes are reeking with purple stains. Again he asks, 'Wherefore art Thou red in Thine apparel, and Thy garments like him that treadeth the wine-fat?' Again the voice replies to his question. The winepress is the visitation of God's wrath: the purple stains are the blood of slaughtered enemies, trampled and crushed under foot by His heavy judgments. 'I have trodden the winepress alone; and of the people there was none with Me: for I will tread them in Mine anger, and trample them in My fury; and their blood shall be sprinkled upon My garments, and I will stain all My raiment. For the day of vengeance is in Mine heart, and the year of My redeemed is come.'

This then is the force of the passage. It is a prophetic announcement of Israel's triumph at the moment of Israel's deepest humiliation; a prophetic denunciation of vengeance on Israel's enemies, when those enemies were proudly triumphing over their prostrate foe. The chief offender, the bitterest and most insolent foe, is Edom, Israel's brother Edom. In the day of vengeance Edom's punishment shall be the greatest, because her crime was so unnatural, her hostility so uncalled for. Though the horizon is now so dark and stormy, though all hope seems to have vanished, though Israel stands alone among the nations, while her enemies are many and strong and unscrupulous, yet there is One Whose arm is all powerful, One Whose aid is never invoked and never rendered in vain, One Who will silence all insolence and crush all opposition, the never-failing ally of Israel, the Lord Jehovah Himself. This reliance on God alone in the absence of all human aid is the leading idea of the passage. Again and again it is reiterated, 'I have trodden the winepress alone. Of the people there was none with Me. I looked, and there was none to help; I wondered that there was none to uphold. Therefore Mine own arm brought salvation unto Me!'

And yet in contrast to the feebleness and prostration of Israel, Edom possessed just those advantages which seemed calculated to secure success in her enterprises, and impunity in her insolence. In two most important respects Edom was favourably circumstanced among the nations around. Her position was strong, and her inhabitants were sagacious.

Edom was strong. Her fortresses were almost impregnable with the appliances of ancient warfare. The most famous of her strongholds, the rock-bound city of Petra, the wonder of modern travellers, is only accessible by one narrow gorge, which is easily defended. The strength of Edom is more than once celebrated by the Israelite prophets. 'Thou that dwellest in the clefts of the rocks,' 'thou exaltest thyself as the eagle, thou settest thy nest among the stars.' 'Who will lead me into the strong city? Who will bring me into Edom?'

But Edom was not only strong, Edom was wise also. The wisdom of Edom was proverbial. When the sacred historian wishes to extol the wisdom of Solomon, he cannot do so better than by saying that it 'excels the wisdom of all the children of the East country,' that is, of these Edomites. 'Shall I not in that day,' writes Obadiah again, 'destroy the wise men out of Edom, and understanding out of the mount of Esau?' 'Concerning Edom,' says Jeremiah also, 'thus saith the Lord of Hosts; is wisdom no more in Teman? Is counsel perished from the prudent? Is their wisdom vanished?' In this land also seems to be laid the scene of that marvellous book, in which human and divine wisdom are confronted, and the perplexing problems of human life are discussed with such profound intuition. The interlocutors of the Book of Job are chiefly, if not solely, Edomites. And still after the lapse of centuries this nation seems to have retained its character. From Idumea came 'that fox,' the second Herod— the crafty son of a crafty father—retaining the peculiar gift of his race, though degrading it into an instrument of licentiousness and cruelty.

Against these advantages of Edom combined, against the strength of the strong and the wisdom of the wise, Israel, fallen and desolate, had one hope, one ally only. But her faith in this ally rides triumphant over all present disasters and all dark forebodings. The prophet's voice assures her of complete victory; and the later history of the nation is the answer to this appeal.

I have explained the passage thus at length, because from very early times it has suffered much from misinterpretation. It has been supposed that the prophet's words refer immediately to the scene on Calvary; that the figure seen approaching is our Lord Himself; that the solitary treading of the winepress represents His submission to the Father's wrath endured for our redemption. I think it will be plain from what has been said, that this view does not at all meet the requirements of the context. I think it will be seen, also, that the image of treading the winepress, till the garments of the treader are drenched with the blood of the crushed grape-clusters, must signify, not the endurance of punishment, but the infliction of punishment. And, if so, we need not stop here to enquire whether in any proper or natural sense our Blessed Lord could be said to endure the Father's wrath when He ended a life of self-devotion by this sublime act of self-sacrifice, which was the fulfilment of His Father's will.

Far different is the lesson which the text sets forth. It is the lesson of dependence on God's help, in desertion and loneliness, against enemies the most powerful and sagacious, amid circumstances the most adverse, despite all the calculations of human foresight. In some respects we cannot apply the prophet's words to ourselves without limitation or correction. The Gospel has supplanted the Law. The Israel after the spirit has taken the place of the Israel after the flesh. The prophet's utterance expresses the indignant cry of an outraged people demanding justice on their enemies, the indomitable enthusiasm of a nation yearning for the restitution of its national life by the mighty arm of the national and yet omnipresent, omnipotent God. To ourselves all men are fellow-countrymen, are brothers in Christ. A larger, more comprehensive, more spiritual conception of God's triumphs is vouchsafed in the Gospel. Our vision is enlarged; our point of view is changed;

but the main lesson of the passage—the heroism of loneliness, the trust in God, the assurance of victory—has the same binding force now as then.

It may be that the interpretation of the passage, to which I have already referred, has led other Churches besides our own to select this passage in place of one of the Epistles in Passion Week. But, whatever motives may have influenced the choice, it is very appropriate for that solemn season. I do not mean only that, as speaking of a redemption, it may be taken to have a Messianic reference, but that it sets forth the very lesson, of which the scene on Calvary was the most signal manifestation ever held out to a sinning, suffering world. The Passion and Death of Christ were preeminently the victory of loneliness through faith in the power of the unseen God. He, Who had gathered about Him admiring multitudes in Galilee, Who had been accompanied from village to village, and from city to city, by eager and attentive throngs, now at length in the hour of deepest trial, in the face of cruel sufferings and ignominious death, was abandoned by all. Loneliness, entire loneliness, only the more painful by contrast with the crowded audiences and the enthusiastic welcomes of the past, was the keenest pang of that painful crisis. In the agony of Gethsemane His nearest and best beloved disciples could not even watch with Him for a single hour.

At the moment of His betrayal one and all 'forsook Him and fled.' And so the cruel taunts of the Roman soldiers, the insolent ribaldry of the Jewish mob, the cold injustice of Pilate, the bigoted hatred of Caiaphas, were encountered and endured without one friendly eye to gladden Him or one friendly voice to console Him ; till at length, when His sufferings had reached their climax, and the agony of death was upon Him, even the Father Himself seemed for the moment to have veiled His face, and in anguish of spirit He cried, 'My God, My God, why hast Thou forsaken Me?' In that awful solitude the triumph over the enemies of God was complete—the triumph over sin, over the world, the flesh, and the devil. For then, when He was all alone, the Almighty Conqueror drew near, with arm upraised to maintain the righteous cause, even as of old He was seen in the prophet's vision approaching from Edom. 'I looked and there was none to help.' 'Who is this that cometh ? This that is glorious in His apparel, travelling in the greatness of His strength ?' 'I am He that speaketh in righteousness, mighty to save.'

And so also it must be with us. Our most heroic achievements, our most signal victories, must be wrought in solitude. With God, and God alone, on our side, we must fight, and we must conquer. There is indeed a solitude, which is due to our own faults, which arises from a cold or churlish disposition, from our imperfect sympathy, from our indolence or our selfishness. We not unfrequently hear persons complain that they are misunderstood or neglected, that no one seems to care for them, that they are very lonely in the world; when they have taken no pains to consult the well-being, or win the affections, of others. It is not of this loneliness that I speak.

But there is also the loneliness of a great moral purpose. A man steps forward as the advocate of some forgotten truth, or the champion of some neglected cause. Or he devotes himself to the reform of some flagrant social abuse, or to the amelioration of some degraded class. The truth, the justice, the expediency, of his cause seem to him very manifest. He sets about his work with high hopes. He feels confident of enlisting the sympathies, and securing the aid, of all honest and fair-judging men. He forecasts a complete and speedy triumph. But his bright anticipations soon fade into the sickly light of experience. He encounters prejudice, ignorance, misunderstanding, the *inertia* of habit and the obstinacy of self-interest, secret obloquy and open antagonism, a thousand unforeseen difficulties lying across his path. Each fresh effort seems to start some new form of opposition. At length, worn out and desponding, he begins to ask himself, whether it is worth while persevering at so much cost, whether he is bound by any obligation to so vast a self-sacrifice, whether success is not wholly beyond his reach, whether he may not be wrong and others right after all, for who is he against so many? Then is the trial of his heroism: then is the discipline of his faith. In this hour of loneliness the prophetic vision will be his comfort and stay. He sees the form of the Almighty Conqueror, emerging from the moral confusion of his soul, from the gloom of distraction and despair. He feels that, though alone, he is not alone. He knows that his victory is secure. He, Who speaks in righteousness, will maintain the righteous cause. He, Who is mighty to save, will rescue him from the perplexity of his position. 'I looked, and there was none to help; and I wondered that there was none to uphold: therefore Mine own arm brought salvation unto Me.'

I will take one more example. It is not now the loneliness of a great purpose which must be worked out without the sympathy of others, but the loneliness of a sinful temptation, which must be fought and conquered in the secrecy of our own heart. For the struggle with temptation, whatever form our special temptation may take, must be, in most cases and at most seasons, of this kind. The companionship of friends, the experience and advice of wise counsellors, the precepts gathered from books, may do something: but at best it will be very little. Our own temptation depends too much on our character, has too great individuality, is too much part of ourselves, to be communicated absolutely and unreservedly to others, even if it were right so to communicate it. The fight must be fought in solitude. The combat must be single-handed. Against the subtle disguises under which our foe seeks to ensnare and ruin us, against the sudden surprises by which he would strike us down unawares, against the harassing doubts which tempt us to elude the combat, whispering that expediency alone has value and that sin is no sin, against the despair of a protracted and wearisome struggle with our worst self, we must fight alone. Alone and yet not alone. We shall have the consciousness of an Almighty Presence, encouraging, sustaining, strengthening us; the vision of the Lord of Hosts, Who triumphs over all opposition, and tramples down all temptation under foot, as the purple clusters are crushed in the winepress. 'I looked, and there was none to help; and I wondered that there was none to uphold: therefore Mine own arm brought salvation unto Me.'

In the lonely championship of right and truth against foes without, in the lonely struggle against temptation and trial within, may this consciousness, this vision, be vouchsafed to us—the vision of Him, Who is glorious in His apparel, Who travels in the greatness of His strength; the consciousness of Him, Who speaketh in righteousness, and is mighty to save.

III.

PURITY OF HEART.

Blessed are the pure in heart: for they shall see God.

S. MATTHEW v. 8.

Trinity College Chapel, 3rd Sunday after Easter, 1870.

AN eminent living writer on ethical and kindred subjects, viewing the matter from without, complains of the misuse which Christians make of the moral teaching of the New Testament. He urges with great cogency that it was 'not announced or intended, as a complete doctrine of morals;' that 'the Gospel always refers to a pre-existing morality and confines its precepts to the particulars in which that morality was to be corrected or superseded by a wider and higher.' He therefore condemns that exclusiveness, which refuses to accept any moral lessons except such as are enforced by the letter of the Evangelic or

Apostolic writings. 'They contain and were meant to contain,' he repeats, 'only a part of the truth; many essential elements of the highest morality are among the things which are not provided for, nor intended to be provided for, in the recorded deliverances of the Founder of Christianity.'

I think that few who have thought over the subject will deny that this statement contains an important truth, though they would wish that the form of expression were somewhat modified. Certainly our Lord and His Apostles do assume an existing code of morals, more or less imperfect. They could hardly have done otherwise. So far as this code satisfied the demands of the highest truth, they held it unnecessary to dwell at length on lessons which were already adequately taught. It was to those points in which it failed, in which any code built merely upon the requirements of society must necessarily fail, that the first teachers of Christianity chiefly directed their attention. And if we would truly understand their meaning, we must place ourselves in their position, we must assume what they assumed, and not attempt to build up their superstructure without any regard to the foundation on which it was laid.

To take an instance of this; the duty to the State, as the writer, whom I have already quoted, observes, and as is well known, 'held a disproportionate place' in the ethical teaching of the ancients—so large a place indeed as to be even dangerous to the moral growth of the individual. It is no wonder therefore if our Lord and His Apostles say but little on this subject. What they do say however, shows, as clearly as words can show, that they recognised in all their fulness the claims of public order on the subject. The restlessness of the Jews in Judæa found no countenance in the teaching of our Lord; the restlessness of the Judaic Christians in Rome was denounced in the language of the Apostle of the Gentiles. 'Render to Cæsar the things that are Cæsar's, and to God the things that are God's'—this is the answer given in the one case. 'Let every soul be subject unto the higher powers: the powers that be, are ordained of God. Whosoever therefore resisteth the power, resisteth the ordinance of God: and they that resist shall receive to themselves damnation'—this is the strong rebuke administered in the other. If therefore politics, strictly so called, do not occupy any space in the sayings of our Lord or in the writings of the Apostles, it is not because their claims are ignored, but because it was rather the ethical function of the Gospel to deepen the foundations, and enforce the sanctions, of morality generally; and only so far to deal with individual elements, as there was some great and signal deficiency in the existing moral standard.

The remark, to which I referred at the commencement, appears to me to be of great importance; and it is the more weighty, because, though having a high apologetic value, it proceeds not from a Christian apologist, but from an external observer, who criticises the ethics of the Gospel with at least a dispassionate freedom.

The fact is that in applying the ethical teaching of the Gospel to ourselves, and indeed throughout the whole domain of Christian practice, we must give free scope to our Christian consciousness. In other words, for regulating the details of our conduct, we must refer to our moral faculty, as refined and heightened by the teaching of the Gospel; we must not expect to find a special precept to meet every special occasion. We must trust to the promise of the Spirit, which Christ has given to His disciples. The pregnant maxim of S. Paul, penetrating as it does into every province in which human judgment can exercise itself, is nowhere more important than here: 'The letter killeth, but the Spirit giveth life.' Act on the literal sense of one of our Lord's precepts delivered in this Sermon on the Mount, from which my text is taken, 'Whosoever shall compel thee to go a mile, go with him twain,' on all occasions, and you will bring confusion on yourself; but receive such precepts as they were intended to be received, as parables or types of the right temper of mind, as corrective of the self-assertion, on which human morality can put no adequate check, which it even tends to foster—in short, take the kernel and not the husk of the precept—and you will produce harmony in your moral being.

I spoke of duties to the State as being assumed rather than enforced in the moral teaching of the New Testament. But it is obvious that this principle of tacit assumption may be and must be applied much further. There are many other valuable elements of morality, on which the Gospel does not lay any special stress, simply because the teaching of common life enforces these with sufficient distinctness, and they therefore do not need such external support. There are some virtues, which a man learns to practise in self-defence. There are others, which society exacts as a condition of membership, having learnt by experience that it cannot hold together without their general recognition. Of the first kind are courage, self-reliance, the assertion of one's own rights, the sense of personal dignity. In these respects the danger is generally on the side of excess rather than of defect; the tendency is to mere self-will, mere self-assertion, to a stubborn resistance and disregard of the feelings, the weaknesses, the claims of others. Of the second kind is honesty, which, though antagonistic to a man's natural selfishness, is yet imposed upon him by the imperious law of the community in which he moves and on which he is dependent. Such virtues as these the Gospel does not ignore. On the contrary, it assumes them as the simplest elements of a moral life. And no denunciations are more severe, than those uttered by our Lord against the religious leaders of the people, who notwithstanding their lofty pretensions had not yet mastered these first lessons of morality. But it is not on such points that its efforts are concentrated. The rough teaching of common life would supply what was needed here. The pressure of social constraint would exercise a discipline, the more effective, because constant and inexorable in its demands. This class of virtues society could understand and could enforce.

But beyond and above these lies a whole region of moral life, on which social restraint, whether as law or as public opinion, or in any other form, exercises no effective control at all. And it is just here that the Gospel interposes to supplement and to superadd. If you analyse the ethical teaching of the Sermon on the Mount, you will find that it is almost wholly addressed to supplying this defect. Its moral aim may be said to be twofold; first, to inculcate the value of motive as distinct from the outward act, the realisation; in short, to teach that for the individual himself the goodness or the badness of his conduct is wholly independent of its actual effects, and springs from the inward intention, and from this alone; and, secondly, to emphasize the importance of certain moral elements, to which no appreciable place was assigned in the prevailing ethical code of the day, and which were, and ever are, in imminent danger of being trampled under foot in the race of life, unless borne up by some higher sanction—such as humility, forgiveness, patient endurance, sympathy with poverty and weakness, and the like. Thus the Sermon on the Mount is preeminently corrective and supplementary in its ethical teaching. It is necessarily so. It was addressed, not to the dregs of society, who needed to be instructed in the first principles of morality, but to the disciples, who certainly accepted and practised the best moral teaching of the day, who were destined to be the salt of the earth, and who therefore must aim at a more perfect standard.

And, if you turn to the Beatitudes, you will find that they, one and all, refer to those moral qualities, of which as a rule society takes no cognisance, and to which it offers no rewards, either because it deals only with external acts and cannot reach motives, or because these qualities in themselves are the reverse of obtrusive, and do not press their claims or clamour for recognition. It is on those who suffer patiently and unrepiningly for the right, on those who are gentle or forgiving towards others, on those who are forgetful and depreciatory of self, on those whose study it is to cleanse and purify their hearts, with whom the pursuit of righteousness is a passion, who hunger and thirst after it, impelled as it were by a strong inward craving to follow it on its own account, and regardless of any advantages in the way of reputation, or of influence, which it may accidentally bestow—it is on these, and such as these, that the blessing is pronounced.

Of these Beatitudes, the one which I have taken for my text most strikingly illustrates what has been said. 'Blessed are the pure in heart: for they shall see God.' It is just here that social morality is signally defective. It will enter its protest against the more flagrant violations of this duty, because they tend to disturb social order, and to introduce confusion into common life. But of purity, in and for itself, it shows in many ways that it takes little or no cognisance. It shows this by the uneven measure of justice which it deals out to the two sexes, by the stern inexorable punishment of such sins in the one, and the almost complete impunity which it offers to the other. It shows it by its worship of the memory of some famous character, brilliant perhaps in literature or in politics, but profligate in life. It shows it by its lavish favours bestowed on some social idol of the day, whose only claim is a winning manner or a brilliant address, whose life is utterly and hopelessly corrupt, in whose heart impurity has gathered around it other demons hateful as itself, selfishness, cruelty, deceit, meanness in all its forms (for impurity always will seek such alliances for protection and sympathy), whose conduct has degraded and ruined many an individual soul, and by their ruin steeped whole households in misery. Of purity of heart social morality does not and cannot take any account. For purity of conduct indeed it professes a formal respect; but not here does it bestow its favours and its rewards.

And in fact no reward, which the world has in its power to bestow, would be at all adequate to meet the case. Material advantages—wealth, pleasure, renown, popularity, influence—these are its best and choicest gifts. But purity of heart seeks not these. Purity of heart breathes another atmosphere, lives in another world, exercises other faculties, pursues other aims. And commensurate with its aims is its reward —not a substantial reward as men regard substantial, but yet very real, because alone satisfying, alone lasting, alone independent of time and circumstance. To the pure in heart, it is given to stand face to face before the Eternal Presence—the veil which shrouds Him from the common eye being withdrawn, and the ineffable glory, which none besides may see, streaming upon them with undimmed splendour. Theirs is the indwelling of the Spirit, that

> doth prefer
> Before all temples the upright heart and pure.

To them is vouchsafed in their journey through life the presence of the Holy Thing moving with them night and day. In the strength of this presence they ride onward

> Shattering all evil customs everywhere;

until they reach their goal and Heaven receives them into its glory; and they are crowned as kings

> Far in the spiritual city.

'Blessed are the pure in heart: for they shall see God.'

And will not even the limited experience of many here witness that such a quest so rewarded is no mere poetical fiction, no idle play of the imagination, but an eminently deep religious truth, of great practical moment to us all? Have you not felt, that according as you have allowed any sullying influence to stain your heart, and to dim its purity, just in the same degree your spiritual vision has become clouded over, the scales have thickened upon it, and the Eternal Presence has withdrawn Himself in a veil of mist, and you have looked in vain and have not found, and your greatest, truest joy and comfort and hope has vanished from you? Was it deceit? Was it selfishness? Was it pride? Was it impurity in a stricter sense, indulgence in tainted thoughts or indulgence in forbidden deeds? Cannot you trace the process, if you will give it a moment's reflection, how the cloud gathered and darkened, till the light is wholly shut out, except that now and then in your clearer moments it flashes in upon you with a painful brightness, piercing through the screen of clouds and revealing to you the depth of your degradation and loss? Or on the other hand can you not bear witness, how each stedfast determination to put away the accursed thing, each renewed effort to cleanse and purify your heart, has brought with it a fresh accession of light, has given you a keener vision of the spiritual world, has removed a film from your eye and a load from your spirit, has brought you joy and lightness of heart, because it has placed you nearer to God and to the glory of His presence?

And, if this is so; if this intimate knowledge of the highest truths is vouchsafed, not to acute powers of reasoning, not to vast stores of information, not to critical sagacity or theological attainments, not to poetical genius or scientific culture, not to any or to all of these, but to purity of heart alone, then surely this should be the one paramount aim of our lives, which we should pursue with the unswerving zeal and enthusiasm of a master passion. If the task is great, the reward is great also. A stern and rigorous self-discipline is the first condition of success. This indeed is not a fashionable doctrine. It is the fashion of the day to assert the claims of individual liberty in extravagant terms, and yet to ignore, or almost ignore, self-discipline, self-renunciation, without which the liberty of the individual becomes intolerable to himself and to society. Remember that the most perfect self-command is the truest freedom; that the Apostle of Liberty himself sets the example of keeping his body in subjection. Do not therefore be led away by any commonplaces about liberty; but assert your legitimate command over yourself and keep it. The discipline which you enforce upon yourself is a thousand times more effective, than the discipline imposed from without. Provide yourself with healthy occupations. With healthy recreations for the body, if you will; but, still more, with healthy studies and ideas for the mind; and, above all, with healthy affections and sympathies for the heart. Seek what is healthy in all things: seek what is fresh and simple and transparently pure and guileless. Avoid all taint of corruptness. Experience has taught you how difficult it is to dislodge a corrupt idea from your heart, when it has once found a place there; how will it recur again and again, even though your better nature revolts against it and you give it no encouragement. There is a fatal vitality about such elements of corruptness. You can recall what is noble and elevating only with an effort; what is sullied and degrading will present itself unbidden to your thought. The law of the moral world is analogous to the law of the physical. Disease spreads apace by contact; health has no such spontaneous power of diffusing itself. Therefore it is of vital importance to shun any tainting influence, as a plague-spot: to shun it in your intellectual studies, and to shun it in your social life. To cultivate self-control, to give yourself healthy employment, and to avoid corrupting associations—these three are conditions of success in the great quest to which you have bound yourself. But another still remains. Cultivate your spiritual faculties by prayer and meditation. The higher parts of our nature, because the most subtle, are also the most sensitive. If our intellectual capacities become enfeebled and ultimately paralyzed by neglect or misuse, much more our spiritual. Here again I appeal to your own experience. Can you not bear witness how very soon carelessness and indifference in spiritual matters tells upon your spiritual nature, how very soon a torpor creeps over it, if you neglect your daily prayers, or if you go through your religious duties in a perfunctory, heartless way; how very soon your whole view of things changes, and you begin tacitly to ignore the importance of spiritual life, perhaps half-consciously to argue with yourself that it may be a mere delusion, an idle fancy, after all? It is just because our spiritual nature is so highly wrought, that it will not suffer any trifling or any neglect. A true instinct leads the poet to represent his pure and blameless knight as laying his lance against the chapel door, and entering and kneeling in prayer, when he starts on the quest which is rewarded with the Eternal Vision of Glory.

Do this, and you will not fail. You will dedicate to God the sacrifice which pleases Him best—the freewill offering of the freshness and purity of early manhood: and He in turn will vouchsafe to you the one blessing which is the fulfilment of your truest aspirations, the crown of human bliss—the vision of Himself in unclouded glory. 'Blessed are the pure in heart: for they shall see God.'

IV.

TWO SOWINGS AND TWO HARVESTS.

Be not deceived; God is not mocked: for whatsoever a man soweth, that shall he also reap. For he that soweth to his flesh shall of the flesh reap corruption; but he that soweth to the Spirit shall of the Spirit reap life everlasting.

GALATIANS vi. 7, 8.

Trinity College Chapel, 24th Sunday after Trinity, 1871.

IT may be a matter of question, what moral defect in the Galatian Church was prominent in S. Paul's mind, when he wrote these words, and what therefore is the exact link of thought which connects them with the context. Are they aimed at the niggardliness of those, who refused to provide proper support for their spiritual teachers, or to extend their alms to a distant Church suffering from the effects of famine? Or are they rather directed against others, who vaunting themselves as spiritual, and professing to subordinate the letter, the ritual, the law of ordinances to a higher principle, yet nevertheless through carelessness and self-indulgence were sinking into lower depths of license than those whom they branded as 'carnal?' Whatever may have been the immediate motive, it is clear that the words have a wider application, and cannot be confined to any one development of the fleshly mind.

This then is the great principle, which the text enunciates. It extends the law of cause and effect, which in the physical world is a matter of common observation, to the domain of the moral and theological, from which men, whether professedly worldly or professedly religious, from diverse motives and by manifold subterfuges attempt to exclude it. It declares that certain courses of action, certain modes of life, entail certain inevitable consequences. It pronounces this to be true in the region of human life, as in the region of external nature, that 'while the earth remaineth, seedtime and harvest shall not cease;' true that men do not 'gather grapes of thorns, or figs of thistles;' true that, where tares only have been sown, ears of wheat will not be gathered into the garner.

I need hardly remind you with what persistency and in how many various forms our Lord and His

Apostles enforce this lesson; that God takes men, if we may so say, at their word, deals with them according to their aims, matches His gifts to their ambitions, bestows on them what they crave and withholds from them what they despise, and thus through and in themselves works out His great purpose of equal retribution. I might point in illustration of this to S. Paul's picture of the Gentile world in the opening of the Epistle to the Romans—the earliest and most truthful sketch of the philosophy of religious history—where the degradation and decay of the heathen is traced to the wilful perversion of their aims and darkening of their hearts, which refused to listen to the oracle of conscience speaking within them, and to the voices of nature responding to it from without, till at length 'God gave them over'—the expression is thrice repeated, as if to designate three successive stages in this relinquishment, three successive plunges in their downward course—'gave them over in the lusts of their hearts to uncleanness,' 'gave them over to shameful affections,' 'gave them over' (last of all) 'to a reprobate mind,' when the light of the moral sense had been utterly quenched, and they revelled in their sin and shame, and the corruption was hopeless, irretrievable, final. This in S. Paul's judgment was the outcome of that 'healthy sensuality' of the Greek, which a modern writer has recommended to our favourable consideration as an improvement on the morals of the Gospel. Judge for yourselves; I will add no word to prejudice the verdict. Is this health, is it culture, is it light, is it life; or is it, as S. Paul teaches, vileness and corruption, darkness and death?

Or I might turn again for an illustration to the parable of Lazarus and Dives. Consider the answer to the rich man, when the retribution came and the plea for mercy was urged too late. 'Thou in thy lifetime receivedst *thy* good things.' This is the pivot, on which the moral of the parable turns. They were *his* good things; the things which were to him the realization of the ends and aims of life, the things on which he had set his heart and for which he had spent his energies. They might not be 'good things' in themselves. Some of them might be positively bad, vicious in their processes and dangerous in their results; though for the most part they would have a neutral character, as instruments, advantages, enjoyments, capable of use and capable also of abuse. But to him they represented the ideal of life. He saw nothing beyond, desired nothing beyond. And he had his desire. God granted to him 'his good things.' He enjoyed them—enjoyed them to surfeiting. Whether they answered his expectations, whether they did not pall on his palate, did not leave a loathing, a dissatisfied feeling behind, is another matter. The point of the parable is this; that, what he sought for, that he attained; that the seed, which he had sown, had borne its proper fruit in its due season, and that therefore no ground of complaint was left. He had sown to the flesh; and of the flesh he had reaped, in the present, indolence, luxury, magnificence, self-indulgence in its highest and its lowest forms; but in the present and in the future alike spiritual corruption and spiritual death.

In the text two great principles are set the one against the other—flesh and Spirit, darkness and light, life and death. And each man is required to make his election between the two. On whichever alternative his choice may fall, he accepts the disadvantages, as well as the advantages, of that alternative. It would be foolish, as it would be futile, to understate the disadvantages of the nobler choice. In the end it will be found true that the yoke is easy and that the burden is light; but a yoke and a burden it is and will inevitably be. And the assumption of this yoke, the shouldering of this burden, must vex and gall, and may even agonize with its unwonted pressure. Yet, if the child that has been indulged in its every whim, that has submitted to no restraints, has learnt no lesson of self-denial in infancy, may even, as a child, have been less happy, because more selfish, than other children, and when it grows out of infancy into boyhood and gets its first rude lessons of the trials of life, may find its position intolerable; if the young man, who wastes his energies and squanders his means and indulges his passions in the vigour and freshness of youth, and thus gambles away all the splendid possibilities of his maturer age, is not a whit more happy even in his present dissipation than his more sober equals, and finds when it is too late that his future is irretrievably ruined—the means which might have started him fairly in life spent, the intellectual endowments which would have more than compensated the lack of material resources stunted and withered by disuse, the whole fibre of his character, his capacity of endurance, his faculty of concentration, his power of self-restraint, wasted in premature decay; then by analogy—as we look forward, no longer from infancy to boyhood, no longer from early manhood to mature age, but from time to eternity, from the life here to the life beyond, from the brief transitory elements of our existence to the abiding and permanent, or in Apostolic language from the flesh to the Spirit—it is only reasonable, only accordant with the lessons of common experience, that he who has staked his all on the earlier phase of existence, has lived in it and for it alone without one thought of the more serious destiny beyond, should, when this destiny overtakes him, be plunged into the agony and despair of those who find themselves suddenly confronted with a new life, for which they have undergone no discipline, with which they have cultivated no sympathies, to which they have made no sacrifices, which is utterly alien to their tastes and their habits. This analogy will lead us to suspect, that he who is wise for the future is not (in any true sense of the word) unwise for the present; that in S. Paul's language 'godliness has promise of the life that now is, as well as of the life to come:' but, whether it does this or not, it certainly tends to vindicate as inevitable the law which is laid down in the text; that in God's moral world the harvest reaped shall be as the seed sown, and that every tree shall yield fruit after his kind. Any schemes of salvation, any views of grace, election, assurance, which fail to take into account this essential element, must be wrong. They are futile attempts to set aside the dispensation of Divine Providence. They are a mockery of God.

'He that soweth to his flesh shall of the flesh reap corruption.' What is meant, and what is not meant, by sowing to the flesh, it is important for us to discriminate. It does not mean paying proper attention to the bodily health, for the health of the body is a valuable instrument in performing the functions of our spiritual life. It does not mean giving suitable recreation to the faculties of the mind; for only by such recreation can those faculties be kept sound and vigorous, and fulfil their part as ministers to our spiritual nature. It does not mean attending to our profession or employment, and thus providing adequate means for our support in life; for without such means independence is lost, temptations are multiplied, and the free exercise of the spiritual faculty is shackled in a thousand ways. It does not mean checking and stunting the natural affections; for without the affections duly fostered and guided aright the spiritual life must wither and die for want of proper nutrition. These things it is not. But to live for the sake of amusement only, to live that you may gratify pleasures of the sense, to live that you may indulge your ambition, or your love of popularity, or your love of display, or your love of ease, or even your love of knowledge—regarded as a selfish instinct, without one thought of using it for the benefit of others and to the glory of God—to live for any or all of these is to live for this life alone, whatever form your ideal of this life may take. This is sowing to the flesh; this will rear and will reap a harvest of corruption.

The Apostle draws a sharp contrast. He speaks only of the two extremes, the two antagonist elements

—flesh and Spirit. But there are whole regions lying between and occupying neutral ground—regions which may be annexed to the one or the other as either becomes more powerful. Let us then interpolate between the two.

'He that soweth to the intellect, shall of the intellect reap'—first of all, intellectual triumphs. Of this he may be assured. But whether the end shall be corruption, or whether it shall be life eternal, this still remains undetermined. These intellectual acquisitions are our business here. They are our justification, as a Collegiate body. If we fail in these, we have not answered our end; we have pronounced our doom. The salt has lost its savour, and it is henceforth good for nothing but to be cast out and to be trodden under foot of men. But, if so, it is only the more incumbent upon us, to ask, whether in this province we are sowing to the flesh or sowing to the Spirit?

For it is not difficult to see, how intellectual gifts and intellectual activity may minister to the flesh, may sow the seeds of corruption; and when this is the case, the corruption will be all the more deadly, inasmuch as the faculties thus degraded are the nobler. 'The light of the body' is the eye.' 'If therefore the light that is in thee be darkness, how great is that darkness!'

For instance, a man may enter upon some intellectual investigation from a corrupt motive. There are some departments of Natural Science which are most noble in themselves, which offer to the physician the largest opportunities for practical usefulness, which open out to the student the widest fields of scientific research. But this man's motive is neither philanthropy nor science. A worse than idle curiosity prompts him. He approaches the subject with a sullied touch; and it rots and crumbles in his hands. Here then he has sown to the flesh; and according to the sowing will be the harvest. In the bitter retrospect, when the curse has descended upon him and he is driven from the garden of his happy innocence, he will confess in sorrow and shame the intense moral significance of the earliest pages of that oldest book—at once the oldest and the freshest of all books—where the simple test of obedience is the abstaining from the tree of knowledge of good and evil, and yet this one prohibition is too stringent for the sinful curiosity which pronounces it 'pleasant to the eyes, and a tree to be desired to make one wise.'

Or, again, take a different instance. Past and contemporary literature will furnish only too many examples, where, through the faculty of imagination, the seed has been sown to the flesh, and the inevitable harvest of corruption reaped therefrom. Better—a thousand times better—never to have risen above the dead-level of mediocrity, never to have left any trace on the literature of your country, better to have lived obscure and died forgotten, than once to have prostituted this, the divinest of all intellectual gifts, to minister to the passions of man, and to plant the seeds of corruption in generations yet unborn. Of all possibilities this is the future which we should most deprecate for any man here—worse than the worst reverses of fortune, worse even than the utter degradation of his own personal character, for then at least the evil may perchance die with him, the whole harvest of woe may be reaped by the sower alone.

Cultivate then, as you are bound to do, your choicest intellectual endowments; but so cultivate them, that they may become also your best spiritual instruments; so cultivate them, that you may lay them down a less unworthy offering at the footstool of the Eternal Throne. He, and he only, that soweth to the Spirit, shall of the Spirit reap life eternal.

This spiritual capacity is the crown and glory of human life. To it all other graces, faculties, endowments, lead up. It is their anointed sovereign, their divinely-ordained consummation. Without it the character is mutilated in its most essential part.

With unfeigned pity you will have looked on some poor idiot, in whom the light of the intellect has been quenched, whose rude physical health seems a mockery of his mental state, who retains the features and exhibits the gestures of a man, while yet the vacant stare and the inarticulate muttering and the loose gait tell only too plainly that the nobler part of man is not there. With some such sentiment of compassion we may imagine that a higher being will look down on one of us, rich though he may be in all intellectual gifts, lavishly endowed with the powers of reason and the graces of imagination, in whom nevertheless the divinest faculty of all—the spiritual nature—is a dreary hopeless blank, crushed out by worldliness, or wasted away by disuse. His great intellectual capacities seem only to point the contrast, and to flaunt and to mock at the vacancy of this higher part.

But this spiritual faculty, in proportion as it is the most precious, is also the most delicate part of our nature. It demands the most careful tending. It will stand no rude treatment. It soon withers away with neglect. Without self-discipline and without prayer its life cannot be sustained.

Not without self-discipline. I have heard it advanced in conversation and I have seen it stated in sermons, as an axiom which is not open to question, but must at once command belief, that self-denial, if imposed for some immediate beneficent purpose, as for instance to enable us to minister to the wants of others, is an excellent and praiseworthy thing; but that when there is no such end in view, it is morbid, worthless, delusive. But is this so? Does reason or analogy or experience lend any countenance to this statement? Can the habit of self-denial be formed in any other way than by repeated acts of self-denial? The Apostle is wont to compare the training of the moral and spiritual character to the gymnastic training of the body. Is not the comparison eminently just? It does not do to put off the exercise of self-denial, till there is a distinct demand for self-denial. You can no more deny yourself at pleasure, unless you have undergone a preliminary discipline, than you can put forth the muscular strength and skill requisite for some athletic feat, without the proper physical training. And therefore I say, if you would live the higher life, if you would sow to the Spirit, exercise a stern discipline over yourselves now. Use the rules and the restraints of this place—the fixed hours and the appointed studies—as the instruments of this discipline. It is only by your willing surrender to them that they will be made truly effectual. This do, and conquer sloth, conquer listlessness, conquer indulgence, conquer self.

Not without self-discipline; but also not without

prayer. Prayer—the communion of the human spirit with the Divine—is the proper food of the spiritual life. How far this is the daily habit of any member of this congregation, is known to himself alone. But if we turn to our public services, is it hopeful, that, when morning and evening opportunities of common worship are offered to all, so few are found to attend regularly, and so many think it irksome if they are required to attend even now and then? Is it hopeful, that when Sunday after Sunday the Lord's Table is spread and you are invited to participate in this supreme act of Christian worship—the last command of the dying Saviour, the truest bond of our universal brotherhood, the most intimate communion between the finite and the infinite—so few respond to the call? And yet, if this College is ever to rise to a sense of its highest mission, it must shake off this spiritual lethargy, and throw itself earnestly into this divine life.

It is impossible to watch the tide of vigorous youthful life, as it streams through our antechapel on Sunday evenings, without feeling what untold possibilities of good have been enclosed within the four walls of this building. Here is a vast capacity, an undeveloped spiritual power, which, duly fostered and concentrated, might change the face of society, might revive a Church or regenerate a nation. And yet—

it is a painful thought—in a year or two all these elements will be dispersed. This generation too will go forth, as in the parable, on their several ways, 'one to his farm, another to his merchandise.' The call will be neglected; the good will remain undone; one more glorious possibility will have passed away. Shall this continue, until the College shall cease to be? Shall generation succeed generation and nothing be done? 'And He said unto me, Son of man, can these bones live? And I answered, O Lord God, Thou knowest.' 'Lord, how long?'

V.

EXCEPT IT DIE.

That which thou sowest is not quickened, except it die.
1 CORINTHIANS xv. 36.

Trinity College Chapel, Sexagesima Sunday, 1873.

THERE is no one in this congregation who will not be reminded by these words of some one moment—the most solemn in his life. He will recall the time when he joined in the slow-paced procession, and listened to the mournful language of the Psalmist bewailing the shadowiness, the vanity, the futility of human life, and stood over the yawning grave, and shuddered at the sharp rattle of the soil on the coffin-lid, and then looked down and read the brief memorial—the name, the age, the date—all that remained to the eye of the varied activities of an exuberant life. And then he turned away, thinking sadly of the warm heart that had ceased to beat, and the bright smile which would greet him no more, and the never-failing sympathy which henceforth he would invoke in vain.

And yet, in the midst of his deepest grief, all is not grief. Underlying the pain of immediate loss is a hope, an assurance, which thrills him with a feeling of joy, almost of rapture. He has listened, and his heart has responded, to the great pæan of victory which the Apostle sung eighteen centuries ago over the last enemy fallen, and which the Church repeats as each time she consigns a son or a daughter —no longer to the darkness of despair, but to the hope of a joyful resurrection. And as personal experience and suggestive analogy and impassioned remonstrance and vivid imagery all contribute in turn to the force and fulness of the Apostle's appeal, his heart and mind are wrought into harmony with the magnificent theme, till he joyfully responds to the final Hallelujah, 'Thanks be to God, which giveth us the victory through our Lord Jesus Christ.'

'Through our Lord Jesus Christ.' It is to the triumph of the Gospel embodied in these last words that I would ask your attention this morning. The description of Christ's work given by one great Apostle is this; that by His appearing He 'abolished death, and brought life and immortality to light.' The thanksgiving to God for Christ's mission uttered by another is this; that 'according to His abundant mercy He hath begotten us again unto a lively hope by the resurrection of Jesus Christ from the dead.' Death vanquished, immortality assured—this, in the language alike of S. Paul and of S. Peter, is the fruit of Christ's epiphany to the world.

I propose therefore to enquire into the significance of these Apostolic sayings; and I do not know any better starting-point for the thoughts which the subject suggests, than the language of the text, 'That which thou sowest is not quickened, except it die.' The difference between death with Christ, and death without Christ, could not possibly have a more striking illustration than in the sentiment which dictated these words. For observe, the Apostle does not speak here merely of death conquered, death annihilated, death put out of sight; but death is retained, is transformed, is exalted into an instrument of God's merciful purpose. Death is no longer an unknown terror, but a joyful assurance. Death is the necessary condition of a higher life. 'Verily, verily, I say unto you, except a corn of wheat fall into the ground and die, it abideth alone: but, if it die, it bringeth forth much fruit.' Christ's death bore fruit in the life of the whole world. Each man's death shall bear fruit in his own individual life. But in both cases alike the divine law is the same, 'Except

C. S.

it die.' Where there is no death, there can be no life.

All external nature, all human institutions, ourselves, our affections, our fame, our carefully devised plans, our solidly constructed works, all are subject to this inevitable law. It may be a question of days or of centuries; but the end is the same. Decay, dissolution, death—from these there is no appeal. All creation groaning and travailing in pain together, seeking to be delivered from the bondage of corruption—this idea is not the feverish dream of an overwrought religious sensibility; it is the practical experience of every day and every hour. And yet, though the fact is so patent, human feeling, aye and in some sense human conviction, is a persistent struggle against the operation of this law. We will not, we cannot, resign ourselves to it. Life, permanent life, is a craving of our inmost nature; life, not only for our own personality—though this is a primary aspiration of our being—but life also for whatever is noble, whatever is beautiful, whatever is good. We cannot endure the thought that such should perish. It seems to be a denial of its very nature, that it should exist for a brief span and then pass away. Between the experience of actual fact then, and the invincible craving of the spirit, there is apparently a direct antagonism. No compromise, no truce, between the one and the other seems possible. It is only when we fall back on the idea in the text, 'Except it die,' that we approach at length to a solution of the problem. Here is the true consolation of humanity amidst the wrecks of an ever-decaying and perishing world. Here is the only reconciliation between the fact without and the yearning within.

I do not know any enigma more perplexing than that the freshness, the enthusiasm, the exuberant vivacity of youth should give way to the dull cold monotony of middle age. It seems as though all that is fairest and most glorious in the human creature were fated by a stern law of his nature to be crushed out at the very moment when it gives the brightest promise; as though the moral life of man were only too faithfully pictured in the growth of the flower or the maturity of the fruit, and ripeness and bloom must be the immediate precursors of corruption and decay. It is a sad thought that the brightness and the buoyancy of youth must be over-clouded and weighed down with the cares and the cynicisms and the distrusts of the grown man; that the freedom of youth must be fettered by the self-woven entanglements of maturer age; that the enthusiasm of youth must be numbed and deadened by the freezing moral atmosphere of worldly experience. It is a sad thought, and it would be an intolerable thought, save for the assurance involved in the words, 'Except it die.' Only at the cost of youth can the grander acquisitions of mature life be purchased, heavy as the price may seem. Only on the 'stepping-stones of their dead selves' can men rise to a higher life, painful and rugged though the path must be.

And so again with human institutions. Grand philanthropic schemes, powerful organisations for the service of God and the good of mankind, societies banded together on principles of absolute self-devotion, projects carried out by individuals at a sacrifice of everything that men commonly hold dear—all these perish in rapid succession. Not the nobleness of their ideal, nor the devotion of their champions, nor the grandeur of their results, can save them from decay. Corruption comes, not seldom comes earliest in the noblest. They pass away, like the fabled order of the blameless king, lest one good custom—even the best—should corrupt the world. Here again, what is the consolation of mankind for the loss, but the law of progress enunciated in the words, 'Except it die?' The institution dies, but the work remains. The example, the inspiration, the idea, develope into a higher life. Over the mangled corpses of dead endeavours and dead institutions—the forlorn hope of history—over the ranks that first scaled the strongholds of ignorance and wrong, humanity presses forward and storms the breach and plants the standard on the surrendered heights.

But these examples, pathetic though they are, will bear no comparison with the death of which the text directly speaks, the dissolution of the natural life of man. We call death a trite theme. Trite it is in one sense. Poets and preachers and moralists and philosophers have spent themselves upon it. Trite it is—trite enough. With every beat of the second's pendulum, almost with every word that I utter, one human being is passing away into eternity. But worn-out, threadbare, this it is not, and can never be. Its tragic interest only increases with reflection: its strangeness grows stranger with familiarity. Is there one even in this congregation of young men, who passes a week, or a day, without casting at least a transient thought—if it be no more—on the time when he will be severed from all the associations and interests of the present, when the studies and the amusements that have attracted him, and the projects that he has planned, and the companionships that he has formed, will be as though they were not, and he will set forth on his last long journey, stripped of everything, isolated and alone? Can any one, whose affections are warm, look on the face of another with whom his life is bound up—of mother or sister or friend—without sometimes thinking, and trembling to think, that the severance must come at length, may come at any moment, when nothing will remain but the memory of a love which was dear to him as life itself? Death is a theme of never-dying interest to us. It has a fascination for us. We cannot put away the thought, even if we would.

And at the present time especially this theme appeals to us with more than its wonted power. During the few past weeks great men have been falling thick on every side. Names famous in government, famous in science, famous in law, famous in literature, have swelled the obituary of the opening year. And within the narrower sphere of our collegiate life too the awful presence of death has been felt. Only the other day we followed to his grave the mortal remains of the most venerable member of this society[1]. While we were laying him, our oldest brother, in his last resting-place, within the familiar walls of this college which for nearly seventy years had been his home, and winter spread the ground with a timely pall of snow—far away, among strange faces and in a foreign land, another member of this

---

[1] Adam Sedgwick, LL.D., Woodwardian Professor of Geology and Senior Fellow of the College, died on the morning of January 27th, 1873, aged 87, and was buried in the College Chapel on February 1st.

body, one of our youngest graduates, was struck down by a fever caught under a semi-tropical sun among the historic ruins of ancient 'Sicily; and the hand of death was upon him, though we little suspected it[1]. Letters came expressing his hope of recovery, sketching his plans for the future, providing with characteristic thoughtfulness for the continuance of his interrupted work here. A few hours later the fatal intelligence was flashed to us, that all was over. Then arrived other letters, still in the same strain, still without any foreboding of the end; a voice speaking to us from the very grave, and thus through the irony of circumstances emphasizing with a novel solemnity the uncertainty of human life.

What lesson does all this read to us? Have we here only one illustration more of that cruel commonplace, the instability of life? To the heathen indeed it could not have suggested any less gloomy thought than this; but to you, who read it in the light of Christ's resurrection, the consolation and the joy and the triumph are there; for the Apostle's words ring clear in your ears, 'Except it die.'

If therefore we have learnt in Christ a new estimate of death, if His revelation, without detracting from the solemnity of our conceptions, has yet

---

[1] William Amherst Hayne, B.A., Scholar of the College, died on February 5th, 1873, at Catania, aged 25.

invested it with a beauty and a peacefulness and a glory unknown before, if in short by inspiring new hopes and pointing out new paths He has drawn its sting—then this is a priceless boon, for which we are bound to offer our perpetual thanksgivings.

And that mankind does owe this inestimable gift to Christ, and to Christ alone, I think it is impossible to deny. An eminent English writer in a famous passage avows his conviction that, if Jesus Christ had taught nothing else but the doctrine of the resurrection and the judgment, 'He had pronounced a message of inestimable importance, and well worthy of that splendid apparatus of prophecy and miracles with which His mission was introduced and attested: a message in which the wisest of mankind would rejoice to find an answer to their doubts and rest to their enquiries.' 'It is idle to say,' he adds, 'that a future state had been discovered already; it had been discovered as the Copernican system was; it was one guess among many. He alone discovers who *proves*.' I know that exception has been taken to this passage; but I believe the statement to be substantially true. I turn to the Jews, and I find that the very chiefs of the Jewish hierarchy—the high-priests Annas and Caiaphas themselves—belonged to the sect of the Sadducees, which denied the resurrection. I turn to the Gentiles, and I find that a Roman moralist treats the doctrine of another world and a retribution after death as an exploded fable, no longer believed by any but mere children. This may be an exaggeration, as such sweeping statements in all ages are commonly found to be. But we may safely infer from it that even the shadowy conceptions of immortality and judgment, which were handed down in the popular mythology, had very little hold on the consciences of men. It seems hardly too much therefore to say that the doctrine was a discovery revealed in Christ. It is certainly true, that as an assurance, a motive, a power influencing the whole mind and the whole life, this doctrine then first took its proper place in the estimation of mankind. If we would convince ourselves of this, we need only compare the inscriptions on heathen monuments and the dirges of heathen poets—the pervading sadness, the bitterness, the despair, the gloom which not one single ray of hope pierces—with the radiant joy and trust which light up the thoughts and the language of the Christian mourner, even in the moments of his deepest sorrow. All history is a comment on the Apostle's bold saying, that Christ '*abolished* death and brought life and immortality to light.'

I am well aware that in heathen times men were found, not a few, to meet death with unfaltering step and stedfast eye and unquivering lip. There were heroes then, as there are heroes now. But this is not the point. The conception of death was unchanged. Death was still a stern implacable foe, to be faced and fought. Victory was impossible; but to be vanquished manfully, to succumb without a tear and without a sigh, this at least was within their reach. At best death was to them a negative advantage: it released from trouble, released from suffering, released even from shame. But no joy nor hope attached to it; for it was an end, not a beginning, of life.

But, it may be said, why should not the analogy in the text have suggested to them the true conception of death? Through countless generations seeds were sown and rotted in the ground, and germinated and sprang up into a fresh and more luxuriant life. 'Except it die' had been written on the face of creation from the beginning. The analogy which held good for S. Paul should have been equally convincing to those who lived long ages before.

This is to misconceive the Apostle's meaning. He does not bring forward his analogy to establish his point. His proof of the immortality and the resurrection of man is twofold. It is first and foremost the fact of Christ's resurrection; and it is secondarily the influence which this belief has had in nerving Christ's disciples to a life of persistent self-renunciation and suffering. Only when this point is established, does he adduce the analogy to meet an objection raised by his opponents, 'How are the dead raised?' Just as the plant, he replies, is developed from the germ of the seed, so also is the heavenly life an outgrowth of the earthly.

It is true that Christian writers have from the very first found in the decay and revival of universal nature types, analogies, evidences (if you will) of man's immortality. But nevertheless it is most certain that these analogies were only felt after the belief was established by the knowledge of Christ's resurrection. Suns set and rose before Christ; seeds decayed in the ground, and plants sprang up before Christ. But what was the impression that these regenerations of nature left on the heathen mind? Why, they appeared not as analogies, not as resemblances, but as contrasts to human destiny. All else seemed to speak of incessant renewal, of continuous life; man alone was born to eternal, irrevocable death. 'Suns may set and rise again,' writes one, 'but we, when our brief day has set, must slumber on through one eternal night.' 'Alas! the flowers and the herbs,' mourns another, 'when they perish in the garden, revive again afterward and grow for another year;

but we, the great and strong and wise of men, when once we die, sleep forgotten in the vaults of earth a long unbroken endless sleep[1].' It was the morning ray of Christ's resurrection which changed the face of external nature, lighting it up with new glories; which smote upon the stern features of the mute colossal image, striking out chords of harmony and endowing it with voices unheard before. The majestic sun in the heavens, the meanest herb under foot, joined now in the universal chorus of praise, proclaiming to man the glad tidings of his immortality.

For just this was wanted to give the assurance which mankind craved. Hitherto it had been a hard struggle between physical appearances on the one hand, and human aspirations and instincts on the other. It was difficult to witness the gradual decay of the mental powers, to watch over the sick-bed and see the bodily frame wasting day by day, to count the pulsations of the heart as they grew fewer and feebler till the last throb was hushed; then to gaze on the relaxed muscles, the glazing eye, the marble brow, the bloodless lip; then to consign the motionless body to the greedy flames of the pyre or the slow putrefaction of the grave, and to know that only a few handfuls of dust remained of what so lately

[1] Catullus, *Carm.* 5; Moschus *On the death of Bion*, 100 sq.

was instinct with volition and energy—to see and to know all this, and still to believe that life could survive the momentous change. But yet there was that within the man which told him that his destiny could not end here. He had capacities, which in this world never attained their proper development or worked out their proper results. He had affections, which were imprisoned and fettered here, and which seemed reserved for a larger scope. He had aspirations, which soared far beyond the limits of his present existence. He could not—do what he would —put away the thought that he had a personal interest in the generations to come; that the future of the world was not, and could not be, indifferent to him. Therefore he was anxious that he should leave a good name behind him, that his fame should linger on the tongues of men: and so by stately mausoleums and heaven-aspiring pyramids, by inscribed tablets and sculptured images, he recorded his stammering protest, that he was still a man among men, that he was still alive. But all was vague, uncertain, faltering.

From this suspense Christ set us free. His resurrection dispelled the mists which shrouded the conceptions of mankind; and where before was an uncertain haze, there burst forth the brightness of the unclouded sun. Truth entered into the lowliest cottage doors. Truth made her home in the hearts of the peasant and the artisan. The feeblest child now grasps the idea of immortality with a firmness which was denied to the strongest intellect and the most patient thought before Christ.

And yet now, after the experience of eighteen centuries, we are asked (as though it were a small thing) to throw aside the miraculous element of revelation, to abandon our belief in the fact of the resurrection, that is, to abandon the Christ of the Gospels, the Christ as we have known Him; and to begin anew from the beginning, to grope our way once more 'through darkness up to God,' to seek to discover arguments for the immortality of the soul. What is this but to stultify the experience of history? What is this but to throw mankind back into second childhood? What is this but to return to the state when even with the gifted few, as it has been aptly said, 'a luminous doubt was the very summit of their attainments, and splendid conjecture the result of their most laborious efforts after truth?'

This we cannot do. Christ has given us the victory, and we will not lightly surrender its fruits. Christ has given us the victory. We know now that death is not annihilation, is not vacancy, is not despair. Death is not an end, but a beginning—a beginning of a regenerate and glorified life. The assurance of our immortality has scared away all the nameless terrors which throng in the train of the king of terrors. One weapon only remained in his hands, and this too has been wrested from him by Christ. The sting of death is sin. This sting Christ has drawn: for He has defeated, and in Himself has enabled us to defeat, even sin. So the last terror is gone. The triumph is complete. Death is swallowed up in victory. And all mankind are bidden to join in the Apostle's psalm of praise: 'Thanks be to God that giveth us the victory through our Lord Jesus Christ.'

VI.

THE ONE GOD AND THE GODS MANY.

'Though there be that are called gods, whether in heaven or in earth, (as there be gods many, and lords many,) but to us there is but one God, the Father, of Whom are all things, and we for (unto) Him.'

1 CORINTHIANS viii. 5.

Trinity College Chapel, 24th Sunday after Trinity, 1873.

WE read in the Gospels that on one occasion, when our Lord was plied on all hands with casuistic problems by those who sought to entangle Him in His talk, He Himself confronted His interrogators with one simple, searching question, 'What think ye of the Christ?'

This question has been repeated again and again by Christian preachers with effect. Speaking to professedly Christian people, they have desired to sound the depths of their convictions, to test the ground of their hopes; and they have seen no better way of attaining this end, than by forcing an answer to the question, often repeated, yet ever fresh, 'What think ye of Christ?'

But the question which I desire to put this morning, and to which I wish to elicit a reply, is more elementary still. It strikes home to the very foundations, not only of Christianity, but of religious conviction in any sense. Before we ask, 'What think ye of Christ?' let us be ready with our reply to the prior question, 'What think ye of God?'

What think ye of God? Is it novel and startling to be addressed in such language? Does it seem superfluous to put this question in a Christian age, in a Christian country, to a Christian congregation? And now especially—now as we approach our Advent Season, when the services of the Church will strike the keynote of patience and joy and hope; now when our eyes are straining to catch the first glimpse of that bright presence, the glory of the Only-Begotten, the Shekinah once more resting visibly over the mercy-seat of God's providence; and our ears are intent to arrest the first preluding notes of that angelic strain, announcing the dawn of a new era, when glory shall be to God in the highest—is it not incongruous, is it not cruel, to ask a question which implies this deep misgiving, to interpose this stern demand as a screen before the beatific vision, to interrupt the heavenly harmonies with this jarring, jangling note?

And yet, when, on the one side, the author of a movement, which arrogates the proud title of the philosophy of religion of the future, lays down as his fundamental maxim, that society must be reorganised, without a king and without a God, on the systematic worship of humanity, and by the instrumentality of this new religion, which is the direct negation of theology, proposes to regenerate the world; when, on the other hand, a scientific leader of the day, whose bold epigrammatic utterances are sure to arrest the ear, though they may not convince the mind and cannot satisfy the heart, warns us against this panacea of the positivist, this worship of the Great Being of Humanity, denouncing it in no measured terms as a gross fetichism and a crushing spiritual tyranny, and then calls us to follow him, not that we may throw ourselves, our temptations, our sorrows, our struggles, at the feet of the Everlasting and Loving Father, but that we may assist him in erecting once more an altar to the Unknown and the Unknowable, thus reversing the lesson which the Apostle taught to the bewildered Athenians on Mars' Hill long ages ago, and signing away by one fatal stroke the glorious acquisitions of eighteen

Christian centuries; when discordant voices assail us on all sides, saying, Lo, here is God! or Lo, there! or Lo, He is somewhere or other! or Lo, He is nowhere; then, I say, we have good reason to ask, whether we will suffer ourselves to be diverted from the old and tried paths, or whether, on the other hand, though there be that are called gods many, yet we have, and we have had, but one and the same God, and that God a Father, in Whose all embracing arms we rest in filial trust and hope and love? If the answer of our hearts to this is clear, prompt, unhesitating, then we shall lack nothing. Then in all our joys and all our griefs, in adversity and in prosperity, in youth and age, in health and sickness, living and dying, we shall feel the strength of His sustaining presence. Then 'though we walk through the valley of the shadow of death, we shall fear no evil;' for He will be with us; 'He is our shepherd;' 'His rod and His staff comfort us.'

When S. Paul wrote these words, it was more than ever true, that there were gods many, who claimed the allegiance of men. By the extension of the Roman Empire the barriers between nation and nation had been broken down. There was a general fusion of thought and of practice. With the native merchandise and with the hereditary customs of distant lands, the superstitions and the deities

6—2

also were imported. Thus indigenous religions and foreign religions were everywhere bidding against each other for popular acceptance. Here it was the grave, stately political worship of ancient Rome; and there it was the artistic, imaginative worship of ancient Greece. Here it was some political conception deified; there it was some power of nature; and there again it was some physical condition of man, not infrequently some vile and degrading passion, whose apotheosis demanded recognition. Here the animal-worship of Egypt presented its credentials; there the star-worship of the farther East clamoured to be heard. Last of all—a creation almost of S. Paul's own day—the latest and boldest innovation had been made; Roman emperors by virtue of their office had received divine honours in their lifetime, and become gods on their decease. Only the other day a self-indulgent, cowardly weakling like Claudius had been translated to Olympus, and there enthroned as a deity; and he who now wielded the imperial sceptre, destined to develope into a very monster of human wickedness, a proverb and a byword to all generations—tyrant, sensualist, matricide—would, it seemed, in due course take rank as a god with his predecessors. This was the result (it is a serious thought) of the highest civilisation which the world had ever seen—when in intellectual culture, in political organization and material appliances, in the arts of peace and the arts of war, human society seemed to have reached the zenith; and in the pæans of her poets and the eulogies of her orators the unrivalled glories of queenly Rome were extolled with never-ceasing praises—this result, this apotheosis of monstrous human vice, this vile parody of religion, this outrage on common sense and common decency.

Truly there *were* gods many, whether in heaven or on earth. In this chaos of conflicting claims, where could the devout and reverent mind obtain satisfaction? At what altar, to what God, were prayer and sacrifice to be offered?

The picture of Athens, as given in S. Luke's narrative, is a type of the state of the whole civilised world at that time. It was delivered over to idols of diverse kinds, some beautiful, some grotesque, some hideous, but idols, phantoms all—mythical heroes and dead tyrants, living animals and living men, human lusts and human ambitions, fire and blood, grove and mountain and storm, sun and star, social institutions and physical endowments—each vying with the other for the adoration of mankind. And some there were, who, notwithstanding this glut of deities, felt that their deepest wants were yet unsatisfied, yearned after a loftier ideal of Divinity; and so when some strange visitation had befallen them, striking home to their hearts and intensifying their religious emotions, vaguely conscious of the promptings within them, and feeling blindly after a more substantial truth, they erected an altar to some yet unrecognised power, dedicating it 'to an Unknown God.'

To a God yet unknown to them; but, Heaven be thanked, not unknowable to them, or to us. Christ came and revealed; Paul came and preached. On that anonymous altar, which had been reared in the forlorn heart of humanity, he inscribed the missing name—the name of the Eternal Father, the One True God, 'of Whom are all things, and we unto Him;' the name of the Eternal Son, the One True Lord, 'by Whom are all things, and we by Him.' With an iron pen, in characters indelible, it was graven on the rock for ever. It might indeed have seemed that in the tumultuous clamour of so many voices this new name would have been smothered and have passed away unheeded. It could never have been predicted— no human prescience could have seen so far—that startled by the accents of that unknown name, and scared by the glory of that new light, this multitudinous throng of idols would have vanished out of sight, and hid themselves for ever, with the owls and the bats, in their congenial darkness.

Yet so it was. The blank was filled in. The secret, after which mankind had been groping, was brought to light; the mystery hidden from the ages, revealed. And men saw, and believed. They could not be deceived. Here was the answer to the vague, mysterious questionings within them; here was the satisfaction to the aching, bewildered soul, which panted to slake its thirst in the fountains of Eternal Love.

And by faith they received the truth. From its very nature it could not be apprehended by sight. From its very nature also it was incapable of demonstrative proof. It was not like those mathematical conceptions, which are the primary conditions of thought; it differed wholly from those physical laws, which we establish by processes of extensive induction. Its proof was not external to itself: its evidence was contained in itself, was itself. Its correspondence with the deepest wants, and the loftiest aspirations, of the human heart was its credential; a correspondence as between the wards of a lock and the notches of a key. It claimed to be light; and, if it was light, then it was truth also. This was the simple test. As light it demanded admission. And the verification of its claim was in the result. To those that believed, *this* was their assurance, that, in their believing, 'power was given them to become sons of God;' to those that believed not, *this* was their condemnation, that 'the light was come into the world and they loved the darkness rather than the light.'

And now, in these last days, the words of S. Paul are again applicable, though in a different way. There are that are called gods, whether in heaven or on earth, not a few. They too are idols, phantoms, though unlike the idols of old. Graven images, stocks and stones, material, tangible gods, these they are not; but wan, vague, fantastic spectres, haunting the dim twilight of thought, fascinating the imagination of men, and diverting their gaze from the contemplation of the truth.

There is first the God of philosophical deism—the most specious and the least repulsive of all these idols. He is One, Eternal, Omnipotent. He is in some sense Creator and Governor of the Universe. So far, there is truth. But He is not a Father. He is a mere metaphysical conception, a necessity of the intellect but not a satisfaction to the heart. He can hardly be called a Person. If He be a Person, He is at least so distant, so abstract, so incognisable to us, that we can hold no personal relations with Him. He is not a Father—certainly not *our* Father—not yours and mine. We know nothing of Him: we can only describe Him by negations. We cannot pray to Him, cannot love Him. He does not love us. It is doing violence to this abstract conception to speak of God as love. God has not spoken to us, God has not redeemed us, God has not given us assurance of our immortality. And so, notwithstanding the concession that God exists, that He is One and Eternal, we are still left alone in the world—alone with our struggles and our temptations, alone with our griefs, alone with our sins, alone with all our vague longings, alone with our poor, aching, unsatisfied, human hearts. We are thrown back on our own despair.

From the God of the deist we descend to the God of the pantheist. Nature is God; nature as a spirit, or nature as inanimate energy—this may be doubtful—but nature in some way. There is no God independent of, and external to, nature. And so we ourselves are part of God; not only the spiritual element of our being, but the emotional and the material elements also, our souls, our bodies, our passions, our vices. Yes: our very vices—there is no pausing in the downward series. Sin is an idle word, an empty delusion. The name must henceforth be blotted out of our vocabulary, the idea banished for ever from our conceptions. Our vices—or what we call our vices—not less than our virtues, are processes of the Divine energy, are expressions of the Divine will. And the anathema of the Apostle must be reversed. Be not deceived—the unrighteous, the murderers, the adulterers, and the thieves, and the covetous, and the drunkards, and the extortioners, these inherit the kingdom of God, nay, these are the kingdom of God. They are—it is the inevitable logical consequence of the theory—they are in God and God in them.

I will not stop to enquire what disastrous effect the worship of this God, if it became general, would have on the moral condition of mankind. I seem to see some faint indication of its effects in past history, where some one energy of nature, such as Baal or Astarte, has been held up as an object of adoration. I thankfully acknowledge that the theory is not carried to its strict logical consequences by those who hold it, that it has not been able to stifle the witness of God, the All-Holy, All-Righteous, All-Loving Father, in their heart, that their moral principles rise above their intellectual belief. But I ask you, sons of God, will you exchange the worship of your Heavenly Father for a religion, that confounds the eternal distinction of right and wrong, and orders you to renounce for ever as delusive those ideas, to which you owe (you cannot be mistaken here) whatever is noblest and best, whatever is most exalting and most energizing within you?

From the idol of the pantheist it is one step to the idol of the materialist—I say the idol, for I can no longer say in any sense the God. Law takes the place of Nature. The spectre of a God, which still remained to the pantheist, has now vanished; and the gulf of atheism yawns at our feet. The idea of sin had already been blotted out; the idea of responsibility, by this time reduced to a shadow, now disappears with it. It is idle, senseless now, to talk of morality. At least, if we use the term, we must stamp it with a value wholly different from that for which it has hitherto passed current. Law—inevitable sequence, fatal necessity—is the inexorable tyrant, who reigns autocratic not only in the domain of physical phenomena, but also in the domain of moral purpose and moral action; not influencing, not limiting our conduct only, but all-pervading, omnipotent, absolutely determining that which we call our will, and forcing irresistibly those which we call our actions. All our language, and all our conceptions, must henceforth be changed. It is as foolish to blame a murderer for his crime, as it would be to blame a stone for falling to the ground. These are thy gods, O Israel! Is this light or is it darkness? Interrogate your consciousness; take counsel of your heart, and so give an answer.

And lastly; the positivist offers for our worship his god, which is no God. He sees rightly that man cannot live without religion; and, having blotted

God out of the world, he is bound to provide a substitute. So he sets up a new idol; he bids us fall down and worship the Great Being, Humanity. What is this but the final *reductio ad absurdum* of atheistic speculation? How can we prostrate ourselves before a mere abstract conception, a comprehensive name for the aggregate of beings like ourselves, with our own capricious passions, our own manifold imperfections—some higher and some viler, much viler, than we are? What satisfaction is there for our cravings after an ideal perfection? What power is there here to convince of sin, to redeem from self, to sanctify, to exalt to newness of life? What consolation in our sorrows, what resistance in our temptations, what strength, what hope, what finality?

And now, that we have tried all these gods many, which have a place in the Pantheon of modern speculation, and found them wanting, whither shall we betake ourselves? Shall we close with the advice which has been tendered to us, as the best which in the present chaotic state of opinion we can adopt; and content ourselves with cherishing the most human of man's emotions by worship at the altar of the Unknown and Unknowable? What altar? What worship? What emotions? If the object of our adoration is unknown, the adoration itself must be blind, capricious, unsteady, worthless. As our conception of God, so will be our worship; and as our worship, so will be our lives. If we deify a bloodthirsty tyrant like Moloch, then his temple will reek with the blood of innocent children: but if we enshrine in our hearts the idea of an All-Loving, All-Holy, All-Righteous God, our Father, then on the altar of a self-denying life we shall offer with filial reverence the sweet incense of holiness and love. It is not a matter of indifference, it is a matter of the utmost moment, what are the theological beliefs of the individual, of the nation, of the age. By their ideas men are most powerfully swayed, and their idea of God is the first and most potent of all.

But you are a Christian. You have never yielded to any of these modern idolatries. You have remained faithful in your allegiance to the God of Revelation. This is well. But have you obscured His glory, have you distorted His image, with unworthy conceptions of your own? Have you indeed seen in Him the Father, the Father of yourself and of all mankind, tender, pitiful, long-suffering (albeit righteous), Who willeth not the death of a sinner, Who would have all men come to the knowledge of the truth? Or have you imposed some narrow restrictions of your own on His Fatherhood? Have you limited His merciful design to an elect few, a small circle to which you yourself belong, and complacently condemned all mankind besides to His eternal wrath? Have you represented the sacrifice of Christ, not as a manifestation of God's love, but as a thwarting of God's anger? Have you in your crude, hard, unscriptural definitions practically denied the perfect unity of the Son with the Father in the Eternal Godhead, adoring one as the dispenser of all mercy, and cowering before the other as the fountain of all vengeance and woe?

Not such the lesson of the text. This one confession, 'We have one God the Father, of Whom are all things and we unto Him,' is supplemented and explained by yet another confession, 'We have one Lord Jesus Christ, through Whom are all things and we through Him.' The Incarnation of the Son is the manifestation of the Father. The life of Christ is the verification of the love of God. In Christ's words and works, in His Passion and Resurrection, we read the expression of the Father's will, we trace the lineaments of the Father's face. And so we no longer adore the Unknown. We know what we worship. We have seen and heard. We may not ignore, and we cannot forget. Henceforth His Fatherly love is an abiding presence with us. Henceforth He is about our path by day and about our bed by night; felt, adored, loved. He is our comfort, our stay, our hope. Holy Father, teach us, strengthen us, command us, use us. Chastise us, if it must be so, that Thou mayest purify us. Kill us, if it must be so, that Thou mayest make us alive. But, whether living or dying, we are Thine. Of Thy love we are assured. In Thine everlasting arms we rest in patience and hope, till the dawn of the final and glorious Advent shall break, and we shall see Thy face, and know Thee as Thou art.

VII.

THE MIRROR OF GOD'S GLORY.

We all, with open face beholding as in a glass the glory of the Lord, are changed into the same image from glory to glory.
2 CORINTHIANS iii. 18.

Trinity College Chapel, 24th Sunday after Trinity, 1873.

A VERY few words will suffice by way of preface to explain the metaphor here used by S. Paul. He is dwelling on the universality, the freedom, the absence of reserve, in the Christian dispensation as contrasted with the Mosaic. He tells us that the character of the Law is prefigured by an incident which occurred at its promulgation. It is related that when the two tables were renewed and God confirmed His contract with His people, the event was emphasized by a remarkable occurrence. The face of Moses shone with an unwonted light as he descended from the Mount. It was the reflection of the Divine glory still lingering on his countenance, as he went out from the Eternal Presence. This light dazzled, confused, terrified the Israelites. They were afraid to come near him. So he veiled his face. When he returned to the presence of the Lord, he removed the veil. This occurred several times. Each time, as he presented himself before the people, the veil was drawn over his face, so that they saw not the radiance gradually waning on his features. Each time, as he repaired again to the presence of the Eternal Light, it was taken off, that the fading brightness might be renewed from the effulgence of the Divine Glory.

Though the details of this imagery present some difficulties, its main lesson, with which alone we are now concerned, is clear.

The Old Dispensation had a glory of its own. This was signified by the light which glowed on the face of Moses. But the glory of the Old was not comparable to the glory of the New. It was partial, intermittent, transitory. It had its hour, and it waned into darkness. Every word of the text points to some feature in which the superiority of the Gospel was manifested. 'We all,' says the Apostle, 'we *all*' gaze on the fuller light of the New Dispensation; all —young and old, high and low, ignorant and learned, priests and people, all without exception and without stint. It was not so then. The people were not admitted to the vision of this glory. The people remained at the foot of the mountain. Moses alone ascended to the height; Moses alone gazed on the Divine effulgence. Of the light itself the Israelites saw nothing. They merely caught a glimpse of the dim, fading reflection, as it rested for a moment on the face of God's messenger, ere it passed away—a glimpse too bright for their aching eyes, but dark indeed compared with the cloudless, peerless glory of the Eternal Light Himself. But the contrast does not end here. 'We all,' continues the Apostle, '*with open face*,' or more literally, 'with unveiled face.' Even this secondary borrowed light, this dim and imperfect reflection was not unobstructed, in the case of the Israelites. They were permitted to look for a moment; and then the veil interposed, the glory was withdrawn. But we—we Christians—gaze unimpeded. No intervening obstacle darkens our view. There is no cessation, and no intermission. Even with Moses it was otherwise. The light came and departed. It faded away and it was renewed again. He went in and went out from the presence of the Lord. But we stand ever before the Eternal Glory: we gaze continually, stedfastly, uninterruptedly. And so the radiance, which lights up our own features, grows ever brighter and brighter, till gradually our whole being is changed; the effulgence of the Eternal Presence takes possession of us: it illumines, glorifies, transforms us wholly into its own likeness. 'We are changed,' says the Apostle, 'changed into the same image, from glory to glory.'

Thus all the expressions are carefully chosen to glorify the Christian Dispensation. One idea alone seems at first sight to jar with the general motive. The Apostle speaks of our 'seeing in a glass or mirror;' he declares that we 'are changed into an image.' Is not this a qualification, a disparagement, a concession, we are tempted to ask? After all then we see only a reflection; after all we do not behold the very thing itself. After all we are dependent on a darkened, confused, imperfect representation of the Divine Original.

A seeming disparagement, but not really so. There are mirrors and mirrors—mirrors which blur and distort and discolour the image, and mirrors which by the perfect accuracy and polish of their surface reproduce the object with life-like exactness. Let us ask then what S. Paul intended by this glass and this image, which represents the Divine Glory to our sight? How, by what instrumentality, through what medium, is the Invisible God rendered visible to us? His own context furnishes the answer to the question. He speaks of some who are so blinded that they cannot see 'the light of the glorious Gospel of Christ,' or, more literally, of 'the Gospel of the glory of Christ,' the Gospel, which exhibits, reveals the glory—the bright effulgence, the heavenly radiance, of Christ—Who, continues the Apostle, is the image of God. Here then is the mirror, the Gospel-revelation; here is the image, the Eternal Son; here is the glory, the words, the works, the life, the death, the resurrection, the sovereignty, the personality of Christ. This mirror we are permitted to face; on this image we are told to gaze; from this glory we are bidden to draw ever fresh accessions of light, till we are transformed into the very image itself, and its glory becomes our glory.

Again in this same context the Apostle recurs to the metaphor. Again he describes the Gospel as the light of the knowledge of God which shineth forth in the face of Jesus Christ—in the face, the person, of Jesus Christ. Yes, He has brought the Father near to us: we look upon the face of the Son, and we see the glory of the Father. Thus S. Paul's idea here is the same as when, in the Epistle to the Colossians, he writes that Christ is 'the image of the invisible God,' or as when, in the Epistle to the Hebrews, the Son is called 'the brightness of the Father's glory and the expression of His person.' The Apostle uses the word 'image' here as it is used in another passage of the Epistle last quoted, where 'the very image of the good things to come' is contrasted with 'the shadow,' as the real and true with the unsubstantial and unsatisfying. It is therefore no confused, partial, distorted, inadequate copy, of which the Apostle speaks. It is the very representation of the original itself. 'He that hath seen Me, hath seen the Father; and how sayest thou then, Shew us the Father?'

It is this thought, which fills the Apostle's heart with thankfulness, and floods his lips with praise— the thought of God brought near to men, God revealed in all His goodness, all His holiness, all His majesty, all His power, in the Person and Work of Christ; revealed not to a favoured few, not to a priestly caste, not to a philosophical coterie, not to the learned or the wealthy, or the powerful or the privileged, not to the great ones of this world in any guise; but to all without exception and without reserve.

And this revelation of the Invisible Father through the Incarnate Son is as extensive as it is complete. It reaches to all men, even the lowest, and it contains all truth, even the highest. Already the New Jerusalem, is seen by the eye of faith coming down from heaven ablaze with the glory of the Almighty; already the tabernacle of God has descended and is pitched among men; already we are permitted to gaze on the jewelled walls and the gates of pearl, and the pavement of pure gold; to bathe in the brightness of that Eternal City, which knows not either sunlight or moonlight, 'for the glory of God doth lighten it, and the Lamb is the light thereof.' It was not so before. God spoke of old in types and figures; He fenced Himself about with restrictions many and various, restrictions of time, of place, of person, of ceremonial. The symbol of His presence, the glory overshadowing the mercy-seat, was withdrawn from the eye of men; the holy of holies was hidden by a veil. But in Christ all is changed. The veil is suddenly rent in twain from top to bottom. The inmost sanctuary is exposed to view. The true Shekinah, the Person of Christ, shines forth in all the glory of its unapproachable beauty and brightness. And we—we feeble, unworthy, sin-stained, death-stricken men—are suffered, are invited, are entreated, nay, are compelled to come in, and to gaze on the peerless sight, till our own nature is changed by the absorption of its rays, and we are 'transformed into the same image from glory to glory.'

To look upon the face of Christ—Christ the image of God, Christ the effulgence of His glory, Christ, Whom having seen we have seen the Father also—this is the priceless blessing, as it is also the terrible responsibility, which falls to us Christians.

And this privilege, this duty, is absolutely without limit. There is nothing in heaven or earth; nothing in science or in history or in revelation; nothing of beauty or of goodness or of wisdom or of power; nothing of creative design and adaptation, and nothing of redeeming mercy and love; nothing in the kingdom of nature, and nothing in the kingdom of grace, which does not fall within its range. I say, the kingdom of nature, as well as the kingdom of grace. For ask yourself what S. Paul means, when he speaks of Christ as the image of God. His own language in the Colossian Epistle supplies the answer. He means not only the Incarnate Christ, the Christ of the Gospel, the Christ Who was born of woman and died on the cross; but he means also the pre-incarnate Son, the Eternal Word, Who was with the Father before all time, by Whom He created the universe, through Whom He sustains all nature and directs all history, in Whom alone He is known and can be known to men.

When therefore we are bidden to contemplate the glory of the Eternal Father in the face of Christ, when the Apostle tells us to gaze on the mirror of His Divine perfection, that we may absorb into ourselves the rays of His glory, no limit is placed to the object of our contemplation.

And the fourfold Gospel, as the record of Christ's

sayings and doings, is the mirror in which this image is to be viewed. The birth, the earthly life, the passion, the resurrection of the Eternal Word made flesh—here is the climax of God's goodness, the very focus of the ineffable glory, which guards the throne of Him 'Who dwelleth in the light unapproachable, Whom no man hath seen nor can see.' Here in the gift of His Son, here in the sacrifice of the Cross, is our light, our hope, our life. We look out on the natural world, and we see much which betokens infinite wisdom and power—beneficent adaptation, creative design, wonderful combinations of beauty and utility; but we see much also that perplexes and dismays—the great waste of life and energies (seeds that produce no plants, and plants that yield no fruit), the reciprocal infliction of pain (creature preying upon creature, and itself preyed upon in turn), physical decay and moral corruption—sin and death around and about us everywhere. These things strike the believer with awe, and barb the taunt of the sceptic. But read such facts, as S. Paul read them, in the light of the Gospel. Contemplate the glory of God's purpose as revealed in the person of Christ. Consider how much is involved in that one act of infinite love; and you will no more question the goodness of your Heavenly Father. Though the awe and the mystery must still remain, you will not doubt (how can you?) that in Christ He has purposed, as S. Paul tells us, to release the whole universe now groaning under the bondage of corruption, to gather in one all things in heaven and earth, and out of discord and rebellion to restore universal harmony and peace.

This then is the very sum and substance of the Gospel. This is the one continuous, progressive, endless lesson of the Christian life—this study, this contemplation, this absorption of the purposes, the attributes, the goodness, the glory of the Father as manifested in the life and works, in the person, of Christ. There is no understanding so mean, and no intellect so untutored, that may not learn its true significance. It is as simple as it is profound. There are depths which the most thoughtful philosopher cannot fathom, but there are heights which the merest child can scale. This is the great glory of Christianity, the glory which filled S. Paul's heart with thanksgiving. It is open to all; it is adapted to all; it is attainable by all. It is theology brought down from the skies; it is heaven planted upon earth. This it is, because we contemplate the glory of the Father in the face of Christ. This it is, because the Son of Mary, the babe of Bethlehem, is also the Son of God, the Eternal Word. The Infinite is brought within the comprehension of the finite. The far-off is far-off no longer.

This then must be the main business of our lives—the study of the Christ of the Gospels. We are constantly warned against the divorce of religion and morality; and we need the warning. No divorce could be more soul-destroying than this. That which God has joined together—joined by bonds the most sacred, and intimate, and indissoluble—it is the rankest of all heresies, the most profane of all blasphemies, for any man to part asunder. But from any such danger the study of which I speak will save us. For in this image of the Divine Glory doctrine and practice meet in one; in this mirror of the Divine Purpose theology and morality are blended together. It is the spontaneous, unequivocal testimony, even of unbelievers, that no better guidance in life can be taken than the example of Christ; that, if a man would learn how to act in a particular case, he should ask himself how Christ would have acted under like circumstances. Here is the morality. It is the highest experience of all believers, that the realisation of their union with God in Christ is the first and last effort, as it is the supreme blessing, of the spiritual life. Here is the religion.

And this study, to be effective, must be real, must be intense, must be personal. It is not the contemplation of the sentimentalist, or of the critic, or of the artist, or of the poet, or of the dogmatist, that will be of any avail. These may affect the feelings, the taste, the imagination, the reason, the intellect; but they do not probe the heart and conscience, and they do not touch the life. The true study is nothing less than the appropriation of the Divine image; the constant recalling, realising, copying, growing into it; till the Divine fascination of its glory possesses us wholly.

So gazing in this mirror, so studying this image, we ourselves shall be changed. This is the only test of the true mode of contemplation. We ourselves shall be changed and glorified—not changed now, as we shall be changed then, when in a moment, in the twinkling of an eye, this corruptible shall put on incorruption and this mortal shall put on immortality; not glorified now, with the incomparable glory which shall be revealed hereafter—but changed nevertheless into the similitude of Christ Who is the image of God; glorified with the glory which He had with the Father before the world was; changed by the purification of our hearts, by the devotion of our spirits, by the renewal of our lives; changed with an ever-deepening change which is a foretaste and an earnest of the great hereafter; changed, as we read that the countenance of that first martyr was changed, when the bystanders looked up and saw his face as it were the face of an angel. For we too, like

Stephen, shall have seen the heavens opened; we too shall have gazed upon the Eternal Glory; we too shall have beheld 'the Son of Man standing on the right hand of God.'

VIII.

WHAT ADVANTAGETH IT?

If after the manner of men I have fought with beasts at Ephesus, what advantageth it me? If the dead rise not, let us eat and drink, for to-morrow we die.

1 CORINTHIANS XV. 32.

Trinity College Chapel, 5th Sunday in Lent, 1866[1].

IN an earlier passage of this Epistle S. Paul compares the career of the Apostles to a scene in a Roman amphitheatre. He imagines a vast concourse brought together from all ages and climes; Greek and Barbarian, Roman and Jew, the living and the dead, dwellers on earth and denizens of heaven, the whole universe of sentient beings, assembled in one countless multitude to witness the

[1] In memory of William Whewell, D.D., Master of Trinity College. Preached on the Sunday after his death, which occurred March 6, 1866.

spectacle prepared for them. Tier beyond tier, they stretch away into the far distance, till the eye loses itself in the dizzy indistinguishable throng, fading at length into a faint haze, a quivering glow, of sentient life. And while they thus broaden out in wedge-like masses into the infinitude of space and time, every face and every eye of this vast multitude is concentrated on the lists below. There at the command of the Omnipotent King, Who presides over the spectacle, drawn forth from the obscurity of the dark prisons where they have been reserved until the given signal, and exposed to the curious gaze of these thronging myriads, the Apostles come forward to do His behest. Chained to the car of Christ, they had swollen the train which attended the victor's triumphant progress: and now they are condemned to the fate of the vanquished and enslaved. Patriarchs and prophets, priests and kings, have fought in this same arena. But the interest of the combat is intensified, the spectacle has reached its climax, as they—the Apostles—step forth last, naked and defenceless, at the Almighty President's word, to do battle with the well-trained and well-armed gladiators of the world, or to grapple with the fierce monsters of ignorance and sin. Then indeed this vast amphitheatre is instinct with eager expectation: the eyes of all are bent down on the impending struggle; some with a savage thirst for blood, some with the scorn of an impartial curiosity, some with tender pitiful sympathy. It is a fearful ordeal; to fight against such antagonists, to fight thus unarmed, to fight under the scorching gaze of this multitudinous throng.

So may we venture to draw out the image contained in the Apostle's words, 'I think God hath set forth us the Apostles last, as men condemned to death; for we are made a spectacle unto the world, both to angels and to men.' Nor condemned as common captives or common criminals only, but as the lowest refuse of humanity, the scapegoats of their race and time, too vile to live, fit only for the cruel sports of the arena, if by chance the wrath of the offended powers might be appeased by their destruction; 'We are made as the filth of the world, as the offscouring of all things.'

Once again, in the words which I have chosen for my text, the Apostle returns to this striking similitude. As he argues against those who doubted or denied the immortality of man, the resurrection from the dead, he appeals to this great, moral spectacle, as the witness of the human conscience to something more real and more enduring than earthly pleasures or pains. 'Why stand we in jeopardy every hour?' Is it conceivable that a man should be willing to die daily; to give up all that makes life enjoyable and to be ready to give up life itself; to contend in this arena of a profligate Asiatic capital, a focus and stronghold of heathendom; to stake his life on the issue of an unequal struggle with the savage monsters let loose upon him, with the concentrated force of an ancient and popular superstition, with the selfish zeal of a wealthy and powerful craft, with the ignorant fury of an excited mob; unless he looked through the near considerations of earthly loss and gain, and saw the heavens opening beyond. Why else should he adopt a course so foolish and suicidal? 'If after the manner of men,' if regarding only transient mundane interests, 'I fought with beasts at Ephesus, what advantageth it me?' If this world be all, if heaven be a shadow and hell a fable, then a sane man cannot hesitate for a moment: 'If the dead rise not, let us eat and drink, for to-morrow we die.'

It is a sublime conception, this amphitheatre of the universe contemplating the struggles and sufferings of a handful of feeble, persecuted outcasts. It would be a bold hyperbole, if the crisis had been less critical, the issues less important. But if, as we believe, this was the turning-point of the world's history, if Christ indeed came down from heaven to bring life and immortality to light, if to the Apostles was entrusted the greatest work which has ever taxed the courage and the energies of man, then the occasion cannot be held at all unworthy of the image.

But though the work of the Apostles was so far an exceptional work, though the image thus appropriate could not be applied without exaggeration to any less signal contest, yet it may be taken in some measure to describe the career of the benefactors of mankind, the servants of God, in all ages. The concourse is still assembled; the lists are still open. The same fight must be fought; the same antagonists vanquished. And according as the crisis grows in importance, as the strain on the individual combatant increases, as the antagonism gathers strength and fury, as through obloquy and contempt and persecution the heroic champion of God fights his way to the right and to the truth, just so far may it be said of him, that like the Apostles of old he has been 'set forth as one condemned to death;' has been 'made a spectacle to the world, both to angels and to men.'

But from this vast bewildering concourse of earth and heaven, let us turn to the little amphitheatre which immediately surrounds us, and concentrate our thoughts on the narrow lists in which we ourselves are 'set forth' to slay or be slain. Even within these limits the assemblage of spectators is sufficiently large and august to awe and stimulate us.

A history of more than three centuries gazes down upon our arena. A gathering of great men, such as probably no other College can shew within the same period—historians, poets, statesmen, scholars, divines, interpreters of law, investigators of truth, preachers of righteousness—a long line of spiritual and intellectual ancestry—witnesses our combats. This may be a matter of honest pride and congratulation; or it may be our deepest humiliation, our darkest reproach. Their name, their lustre, their example, are our inheritance; to drag in the dust, or to crown with fresh glory. In the presence of this silent concourse of the past we are called forth by God to do battle for Him.

One honoured name has been recently withdrawn from the lists of the combatants, and added to the ranks of the spectators. Our grand old Master—our pride and strength—has passed from us to them. It is very hard to realise the change. His vacant stall, our mourning badges, speak to us in vain. We can think of him only as we saw him, not so very many days ago, still buoyant and vigorous and full of life; 'his eye not dim, nor his natural force abated;' his step still firm and his carriage erect as ever. All, who observed him of late, rejoiced to see that the shadow which had darkened the last year of his life was passing off. Old studies thrown aside were taken up again. Old interests blunted by sorrow were recovering their keen edge once more. Time seemed only to have mellowed and ripened his character, without decaying his faculties. The screen, which long had hidden his large capacity of affection and strong yearning for sympathy, known to a few and suspected by many more, was falling away. And he, whom all admired and respected, was becoming every day better known and more endeared to all.

By all members of this College far and wide, even by those to whom he was personally unknown, his death will be felt as a personal loss. To us here it has left a sense of vacancy, which before it occurred we could hardly have imagined. So many various interests were linked with his name. So many cherished associations are buried in his grave. His removal seems like a great severance from the past.

Even if he had not risen to any special eminence, still by his unbroken residence of more than fifty years in the College, and by his high position as ruler of our little commonwealth, he would have been so intimately associated with the every-day thoughts and acts, would have occupied so large a space in our memory, that his death must have been deeply felt. But he was recognised by all as no common man. If we are inclined to distrust our own estimate,

S—2

as the partial expression of College pride, in this instance at least the appeal to a larger public will not reverse our verdict. In his published works he has covered a wider field than any living writer; and those, who have conversed with him in private, record with wonder his familiar acquaintance with the farthest outlying regions of knowledge in its lower as well as in its higher forms. What value will be attached by after-ages to his various literary and scientific works, it would be vain to predict; but this at least we may say, that in his own generation and country he has held the foremost rank, if not in precision, at least in range and vigour of intellect.

And these great powers he consecrated always to the highest ends. He is ever a religious teacher in the truest sense. One strain runs through all his works; one cord threads together his earlier and later writings; the days of his literary life are 'bound each to each by natural piety.' The world of matter without, the world of thought within, alike speak to him of the Eternal Creator, the Beneficent Father. These are the strophe and antistrophe of the sublime chorus of Nature; the two witnesses who prophesy before the throne of the God of Revelation. If with the Psalmist he tells how 'The heavens declare the glory of God and the firmament sheweth His handywork,' with the Psalmist also he passes on from the outward witness of creation to the inward witness of the heart, 'The law of the Lord is an undefiled law converting the soul, the testimony of the Lord is sure and giveth wisdom to the simple.' The evidences of Natural Theology formed the subject of his earliest writing by which he became widely known, his Bridgewater Treatise. And this same chord he struck in his last sermon preached in this Chapel not many days before his fatal accident; when choosing a theme strangely prophetic, as it seems now, of his approaching death, and speaking of Him 'Who is the Alpha and Omega, the beginning and the ending,' he passed on from the creation of the world to its dissolution; and in words of striking force thus painted the great and final crisis; 'No mountains sinking under the decrepitude of years or weary rivers ceasing to rejoice in their courses;' 'No placid euthanasia silently leading on the dissolution of the natural world.' 'But the trumpet shall sound; the struggle shall come. This goodly frame of things shall expire amid the throes and agonies of some fierce and sudden catastrophe. And the same arm that plucked the elements from the dark and troubled slumbers of their chaos shall cast them into their tomb[1].'

---

[1] From a Sermon preached on Quinquagesima Sunday, Feb. 11th, 1866, upon the text Rev. i. 8.

On such subjects he wrote often: sometimes with startling boldness, but always with deep reverence. Indeed his tone seems to rise in solemnity, as his speculations grow more daring; for what nobler passage can be shewn in poet or philosopher or divine, than the majestic language in which, speaking of the 'waste' of Creation, he suggests that the other bodies of the universe are 'rolled into forms of symmetry and order, into masses of light and splendour, by the vast whirl which the original creative energy imparted to the luminous elements out of which they were formed;' and describes the planets and stars as 'the lamps which have flown from the potter's wheel of the Great Worker; the shred-coils which in the working sprang from His mighty lathe; the sparks which darted from His awful anvil when the solar system lay incandescent thereon; the curls of vapour which rose from the great cauldron of Creation when its elements were separated[1].'

But while the world without will judge him only by his writings, on our gratitude he has other and stronger claims. During the last quarter of a century, in which he has ruled over us, the College has enjoyed almost unexampled prosperity. How far this is due to the greatness of his name and the generosity of his administration, it would not be easy

[1] *Plurality of Worlds*, pp. 365, 366.

to decide. But after making all allowance for the fond partiality of a recent regret, we may fairly say that as a Master of the College he stands out preeminent in the long list of three centuries; as a man of letters, greatest of all since Bentley; as a munificent and patriotic ruler, greatest of all since Nevile; but, as uniting in himself many and various qualifications which combined go far towards realising the ideal head of a religious and learned foundation, the just representative of a famous academic body, greater than these or any of his predecessors. Vast and varied mental powers, untiring energy and extensive knowledge, integrity of character and strictness of example, a wide and generous munificence, a keen interest in University progress, an intense devotion to his own College, a strong sense of duty, a true largeness of heart, a simple Christian faith; the union of these qualities fairly entitles him to the foremost place among the Masters of Trinity.

For he was most truly our own; our own by long residence, our own in all his feelings and interests, our own in his passionate love for the place. He has been heard to say that the sky always seemed to him brighter, when framed by the walls and turrets of our Great Court; and in his dying hours he desired to have the blinds raised, that he might look once more on this familiar scene, so fair and pleasant to his eyes. This touching incident of his last illness is typical of his whole life. All the currents of his being seemed to set towards this one channel. He delighted to connect the incidents of his domestic life with the College. He inspired his private friends with his own enthusiasm for the College. He was very proud of Trinity, and Trinity was very proud of him.

Our own always; not in his triumphs only, but in his sorrows also. I cannot forget—I do not think that any one who saw him can forget—how on this same Sunday a year ago, in the earliest hours of loneliness, in the first flush of grief, he appeared in this Chapel to join his prayers with ours, rightly judging this the fittest place for the weary and heavy-laden, not shrinking from us as from strangers, nor fearing to commit to our sympathies the saddest of all sad sights, an old man's bereavement and a strong man's tears.

I have spoken of his College feeling; but College feeling with him was not a proud isolation, a repulsive narrowness. If he represented the College, he represented the University not less truly. His College was to him only the centre and focus from which his interest radiated. As in his last princely bequest to the University[1], so in all the acts of his academic life,

---

[1] This refers to a provision of Dr Whewell's will, whereby property (of which the estimated value was between £60,000 and

he regarded Trinity College as holding a great trust for the benefit of that larger body of which it forms a part, from which it derives strength, and to which it communicates strength in turn.

He has gone from us, leaving as a legacy his name and his munificence. He has bequeathed to us also his bright example. His race is run: his torch has passed into our hands full burning; to keep ablaze or to quench, as we will. In intellectual eminence we cannot follow him. But the moral qualities, which clustered about his mental power, may be imitated even by the least gifted among us. The unflagging energy which overcame all disadvantages, the manly courage which ever disdained unworthy applause, the simple faith in God through Christ which in him was thrown into stronger relief by his large acquaintance with all branches of human knowledge; such qualities as these are not beyond the reach of any. His example supplies a fresh incentive, as it imposes a fresh responsibility.

The Master's death occupies the first place in our thoughts. But this is not the only loss we have

£70,000), consisting of the site and buildings opposite Trinity College, together with all the residuary personalty, was conveyed in trust to the College, for the purpose of providing accommodation for its members, and of founding and endowing a Professorship and Studentships of International Law in the University.

sustained during the last fortnight. While we were committing his remains to their final resting-place, an older contemporary—a gentle and loving spirit—was passing silently away. He too, though unknown to most of us, had spent the best part of his life in this place, and devoted his freshest energies to the College. He was a scholar, as those bear witness who heard him here, 'a ripe and good one;' but he was very much more than a scholar. As a Tutor of this busy College, and as a parish clergyman in his quiet northern home, he was one and unchanged; the same pure, single-hearted, blameless man, humble and childlike, loving and loved by all. His words were the counterpart of his deeds; his books the reflection of his life. In the Rectory of Valehead and the Bishopric of Souls was traced the unconscious portrait of the Vicar of Heversham[1].

As each successive combatant is withdrawn from the lists, as we lay first one and then another in an honoured grave, the question will rise in our hearts, 'To what end are these well-fought battles, these

---

[1] Robert Wilson Evans, B.D., formerly Fellow and Tutor of Trinity, and sometime Archdeacon of Westmoreland, died on Saturday morning, March 10th (the day of Dr Whewell's funeral), aged 76. At the time of his death he held the vicarage of Heversham, in the gift of Trinity College, to which living he was instituted in 1842.

hardly-won victories?' If true life is, as not only the Christian Apostle but even the Stoic philosopher[1] called it, a warfare; if men praise and honour most after death those who in their lifetime grappled with difficulties, conquered unruly passions in themselves, subdued ignorance and vice in others, faced misunderstanding or endured persecution; if we strive by their example to nerve ourselves for the same arena in which they have fought before; should we, or rather can we, refrain from asking for them and for ourselves, 'What advantageth it?'

To this question the Apostle saw one answer only. It is difficult to conceive any other. If the dead rise not, then these unselfish struggles, these lifelong labours, are mere vanity; then the world's chief benefactors are its greatest losers. It is folly to forego present advantage, to incur present reproach, to sacrifice this life, if there is no life beyond the grave. Then it were better, like those reckless citizens of Judah, who in the presence of a dangerous foe gave themselves up to feasting and revelry, to live only for the moment and cast no thought beyond; then the motto adopted by them and by pleasure-seekers in every age is after all the golden rule of life; 'Let us eat and drink; for to-morrow we die.'

For, though we stifle the voice, it will still make

[1] Seneca, *Epist.* 96, 'vivere militare est'.

itself heard. Humanity cannot be thus forcibly repressed. A religion or a philosophy, which neglects this elemental instinct of our nature, which holds out no rewards, stands self-condemned. It is an irresistible impulse which leads to the question, 'What advantageth it?' which suggests the train of thought, 'Why stand I in jeopardy every hour?'

And yet a voice equally clear proclaims in still more commanding tones, that self-denial is better than self-indulgence; that it is noble and good to devote ourselves to the advancement of truth and to works of love; that it is noblest and best of all to pursue this course in the teeth of opposition and obloquy, 'enduring the cross and despising the shame,' reaping no reward on this side the grave. We cannot call such men fools; we respect and admire them; we desire to be like them; we envy their courage, their perseverance, their lofty self-devotion.

The resurrection of the dead, the life to come, is the only solution of the perplexity, the sole harmonizer of these two conflicting voices. And accordingly, as the human race progressed in culture, as the moral faculties were more fully developed, the doctrine of man's immortality became more and more prominent.

Yet still it remained a speculative opinion, a vague yearning, a shadowy hope. At length the signal was vouchsafed. The Son of Man rose from the grave.

The doubtful hypothesis became an accredited fact, the settled belief of distant nations, the entailed inheritance of successive ages. To the perplexing question, 'What advantageth it?' a full and final answer was given, 'Now is Christ risen from the dead, and become the first-fruits of them that slept.'

With this assurance he, whom we mourn to-day, lived and laboured and died. With this assurance we laid him in his grave, looking forward to a joyful resurrection. With this assurance let us all—young and old—now devote ourselves anew to the service of God in Christ, recalling our baptismal pledges and resolving, as far as in us lies, to make this College a Holy Temple of His Spirit in all sound learning and all godly living.

PREACHED
BEFORE THE UNIVERSITY,
1868—1883.

I.

SHEW US THE FATHER.

Philip saith unto Him, Lord, shew us the Father, and it sufficeth us. Jesus saith unto him, Have I been so long time with you, and yet hast thou not known Me, Philip? He that hath seen Me, hath seen the Father; and how sayest thou then, Shew us the Father?

S. JOHN xiv. 8, 9.

Great S. Mary's Church, Advent Sunday, 1868.

THE opening of S. John's Gospel speaks of One, Who has been with God from eternity, Who is God Himself. This Being, so described, the Evangelist calls the Logos—the Divine Reason, the Divine Word. He is the Divine Reason, for He is the expression of God's will in the creation and government of the Universe. He is the Divine Word, because through His operations alone God reveals Himself, God speaks, as it were, to our finite capacities. This Word of God is His Agent in all His words and works, howsoever and whensoever He manifests Himself. This is no less true of the natural world, than of the spiritual world. All things were created, all things are sustained, through Him. Here is the Evangelist's starting-point. And having thus with eagle eye swept the whole field of the Universe in one comprehensive glance, he gradually narrows his range of view and concentrates his gaze, until it is fixed on the very focus of light, the visible presence of the Shekinah on earth, the Incarnation of this Word of God.

(1) First, from the material creation he passes to the intellectual and moral creation. Whatsoever of knowledge, whatsoever of wisdom, whatsoever of invention, whatever discernment of physical facts, whatever insight into human affairs, whatever yearning after heavenly truths, has been vouchsafed to mankind in any age—to the savage in the first dawn of intellect and conscience, and to the sage in the full noontide blaze of his heightened faculties—all these, the first germ and the latest development, are the gift, are the indwelling, of the Divine Word. He is 'the life,' and He is 'the light of men.' The mental and moral growth of individuals and societies and nations alike are due to Him. He originates, He inspires, He developes, He ripens into maturity. His

dominion is as complete in the region of mind and spirit, as in the region of physical growth and physical change.

(2) This—the passage from the material to the moral and intellectual world—is the first stage in the Evangelist's progress towards his goal, the first contraction, the first intensification, of his vision. And then comes another.

This Word of God has indeed illumined and quickened all men and all races in their several degrees, Buddha and Confucius and Zoroaster, Zeno and Pythagoras, Indians and Persians, Babylonians and Egyptians, Greeks and Romans. He has been present in universal history, as He has been present in every individual soul of man. But nevertheless He has specially visited one family, one race. There was a prerogative tribe selected in due time from the rest, a firstfruits of the nations of the earth, a peculiar people consecrated to God. Though there be many tributaries, the main stream of religious history runs in this channel. To this nation the Word of God came as to His own inheritance, spake as to His own household—spake by lawgivers and prophets, by priests and kings, spake in divers stages and divers manners, spake with an intensity and a power and a directness, with a continuity and a fulness, with which He spake to no other nation besides. In neither case was the response equal to the appeal. Among the nations at large 'the light' shone 'in the darkness, and the darkness comprehended it not:' to the descendants of Abraham 'He came as to His own' vineyard; yet 'His own received Him not.' Nevertheless among both—among the nations whom He approached through the avenues of the natural conscience, and among the Israelites to whom He spake in the piercing tones of Inspiration, there were those who did feel His presence, did hear His voice; and these were rescued from their grovelling, material, earthly life, were born anew in Him, were made sons of God through God the Word.

(3) And having thus passed by successive stages first from the physical world to the moral world, from universal nature to universal history, and next from universal history to the records of the one prerogative race, the Evangelist lastly concentrates our thoughts on a single incident in these records, a single link in the chain of the Divine dispensation. He has just directed us to the one conspicuously bright *line* which traverses the plane of the world's history; and now he guides our eye along this line, till it is arrested at one intensely brilliant *point*, in which are concentrated the illuminating rays of the Word of God, which is the focus of the spiritual development of mankind. The Word, Whose voice was not unheard even by

Gentiles, Who spoke still more clearly in the writings of the Old Covenant and the career of the chosen people, 'was made flesh and dwelt among us'—not only spoke through man, but identified Himself with man. The dream of Jewish doctors, who looked forward to the advent of Messiah's kingdom, the day of redemption when the Divine glory should rest once more on the mercy-seat, was here fulfilled, though they discerned it not. The Shekinah was restored once more to the Temple. The bright light—brighter far than of old—did rest once more over the Sanctuary. The Word of God 'tabernacled' among men. 'And we,' adds the Evangelist, the beloved disciple, the familiar friend of the Word Incarnate, speaking with the intensity of a strong, unchangeable, personal conviction, 'we beheld His glory, the glory as of the only-begotten of the Father.'

Such is the Divine philosophy of creation and history and religion, as sketched by the pen of S. John. He views the Gospel of Christ, the Incarnation of the Son of God, not so much in contrast, as in connexion, with the natural heavenward aspirations of man, with the other religions of the world. The Incarnation is not an isolated fact, not the one only operation of the Divine Word. It is indeed unique, is paramount, does transcend, far transcend, all other operations. The lesson is higher, but still the Teacher is the same. It is the explanation of the past, the culminating point of human history, the consummation of God's revelation to man. For now first the Divine and the human are united in immediate and inalienable contact. But it does not stand alone; nor does it profess an affinity only with the Jewish dispensation. God has revealed Himself also in nature and in history, in the workings of the individual conscience and in the education of the whole race. The folds of the veil in each case may be more or less dense. But to those who have eyes to read and hearts to understand, though it may partially screen, it cannot conceal, the Divine Presence behind, the awful majesty of the Eternal Father. And I cannot but express my own strong conviction that, if Christian apologists and Christian divines were more ready to accept the teaching of S. John in this respect, and to survey the religions of the world from the commanding ground which he has marked out for them; if, instead of accentuating the contrasts and dwelling only on the follies and wickednesses, they would investigate more diligently and recognise more gladly the elements of the Divine teaching in all, even the more degraded, forms of heathen worship; if they would track out the foot-prints of the Word of God impressed now faintly, and now more vividly, on the sands of universal history, they would find not only that numberless objections to Christianity founded on the partial resemblances, the imperfect graspings after truth, in other religious systems, would melt away in the process, but that a flood of new light would at the same time be shed upon the significance and the power of the Gospel.

It was not however with any intention of dwelling at length on this general question, that I have thus called attention to the main bearing of the opening paragraphs of S. John's Gospel. But this introduction is the key to the meaning of the whole narrative. Our Lord's words related therein require to be read by the light of this prologue, if we would enter into their full meaning. They are the utterances not only of Jesus the Deliverer, the Redeemer of His people, the long-expected Christ of Israel; but they are the utterances also of the very Word of God, Who was in the world from the beginning, and now in these last days speaks to men in the flesh.

So it is with the expression in the text. The Master has just foretold to His little band of followers, that He and they must soon part. With this severance in view He bids them cling closer to one another, love one another as brothers. He warns them that He must go alone, that they cannot follow Him. The announcement fills their hearts with dismay. He seeks to allay their sorrow. Let them trust in God. He is going to prepare an abode for them. He will come again, and take them home with Him. 'Whither I go,' He adds, 'ye know, and the way ye know.' Thomas here breaks in, doubtful and desponding as ever. Half reproachfully he asks, 'Lord, we know not whither Thou goest, and how can we know the way?' Then Jesus declares Himself to be the Way, the only Way, to the Father. Knowing Him, they must know the Father. 'And,' He adds, 'henceforth ye know Him, and have seen Him.'

It is not now Thomas, but Philip, who takes up the conversation—a different man and a different temper. In the records of the other Evangelists, Philip the Apostle is a name only. In S. John's Gospel, he appears as something more than a name, as a well-defined character. Very early tradition represents him in later life residing in Asia Minor, in the same region as the beloved disciple himself. It may be therefore that the Evangelist had local reasons for dwelling on those few incidents in which Philip takes a prominent part. At all events, few though they are, these incidents seem to reveal the man's character very clearly. His is a precise, careful, matter-of-fact mind. He is wanting in spiritual insight, but he is prompt and ready in action. It may be, as some have thought, that he was the steward of the little company, just as Judas was the treasurer. If so, we have an easy explanation of the fact that our Lord puts to him the question how the five thousand are to be fed. If so, again, we may see how on another occasion some Greeks, when they wish to obtain access to our Lord, would naturally come in contact with him, and address themselves to him first. At all events, whether or not he had a business vocation connected with his discipleship, he had at least a business turn of mind. There is a precision and minuteness in the few sentences ascribed to him by the Evangelist, which cannot be quite accidental. 'We have found Him, of Whom Moses in the law, and the prophets, did write, Jesus of Nazareth, the son of Joseph.' 'Two hundred pennyworth of bread is not sufficient for them, that every one of them may take a little.' He is anxious for himself, and he is anxious for others, that everything should be subjected to the faithful testimony of the eyes. In answer to Nathanael's question in the opening of the Gospel he says eagerly, 'Come and *see*.' In reply to our Lord's declaration in the text, it is his first impulse to seek ocular proof, '*Shew* us the Father, and it sufficeth us.' A very ancient tradition relates that this Philip was the disciple who in another Gospel pleads, 'Lord, suffer me first to go and bury my father,' and is answered by the rebuke, 'Let the dead bury their dead; but go thou and preach the kingdom of God.'

This tradition is true to character, and I can well believe it true to fact. It is not so much the request, as the temper which dictates the request, that our Lord there rebukes. And such a temper is Philip's.

'Only let us *see* the Father,' he says, 'and we ask nothing more. Then there will be no more hesitation, no more vagueness, no more cowardice, no more repining. This will console us, will strengthen us, will inspire us. We shall not shrink from being left alone. We shall bear our severance manfully, cheerfully. We shall be ready to do and to suffer anything. Vouchsafe us one glance, one glance only. We ask nothing more. To see is to believe.'

The demand may be made, and doubtless is made, in many different tempers. There are those who, like Philip, make it in the earnest desire to find a surer standing-ground for their faith, who eagerly wish to dispel the last shadow of doubt, who are prepared to follow up their belief, once confirmed, are ready to live and to die for it. Only they must first be certified, must first have seen. There are others who, consciously or unconsciously, have persuaded themselves that by the mere act of making the demand they have thrown off a load of responsibility, that, until they get an answer, they are free to act as they like, free to live as though there were no Father in Heaven, because they do not see Him. And, lastly, there are some who make it in a temper directly opposed to Philip's, who demand to be shewn the Father in the same spirit in which Pilate asked to know, 'What is truth?' mocking while they interrogate and determined to accept no reply. Or they refuse to make the demand at all, because they have persuaded themselves that it is an absurdity. There is a dark, impenetrable veil, they say, separating the seen from the unseen, the world of sense from the world of spirit. At least there is a dark, impenetrable veil; but whether it conceals anything or nothing, they do not care to ask. It may, or it may not, screen the awful form of an Eternal, loving Father. It may, or it may not, separate us from a life of immortality, a world of spirits, a heaven of bliss. You cannot raise the veil; you cannot see through it. It is easier, better, wiser to desist from the attempt—to rest content to play your little part on this world's stage creditably and comfortably, and to leave the rest—not to faith, not to God: here would be the old delusion again—but to blind chance, to blank uncertainty.

But in whatever temper men may make the demand—in eagerness or in apathy or in mockery—the fundamental error is still the same. They look for a kind of proof, which the subject does not admit. They appeal to organs which are not cognisant of spiritual things. If it is not by the senses, so neither is it by theological and scientific faculties, that we can apprehend God, can see the Father. These faculties may verify, may explain, may systematize; but they cannot give the insight, cannot create the belief. I doubt whether the most elaborate proofs of the being and attributes of God, the most subtle expositions of the evidences of Christianity, have done very much towards establishing even an intellectual assent. I am quite sure they have been all but powerless in commanding a living, working belief. It is by the Spirit alone that spiritual truths are discerned. 'Eye hath not seen, nor ear heard...but God hath revealed.' Every man has this spiritual faculty. He may deal with it, as he may deal with any other faculty. He may enfeeble it by disuse, he may crush it by main force: or he may educate and quicken and intensify it. And according as he does the one or the other, so will be his spiritual insight, his consciousness of the Father's presence.

And this is the force of our Lord's reply in the text. 'Have I been so long time with you, and yet hast thou not known Me, Philip? He that hath seen Me, hath seen the Father; and how sayest thou then, Shew us the Father?' You ask for an external, tangible demonstration which will not, which cannot, be granted to you. You entirely mistake the nature of the knowledge which you seek, of the means by which it is attained. Meanwhile all the elements of this knowledge are open before you. The Father has unveiled His face to you, and you have not seen Him. In His Word throughout all ages, in His Word incarnate in these latter days, He has spoken to you, and you have not heard Him. Now for these three years He has shewn Himself to you twelve men, as He has never shewn Himself before. And this is the end, this is the misapprehension even of those to whom His glory has been most fully and nearly revealed—this dissatisfaction, this blindness, this ignorance, this demand, 'Shew us the Father?'

To ourselves, as to Philip, the rebuke is addressed. 'Have I been so long time with you, and hast thou not known Me—not known Me, the Word of God, Whose seal is set on all nature and all history; not known Me, the Incarnate Son, Whose personal ministry is written in the Gospels, and Whose name is stamped on the life of the Church?'

And now on this Advent Day, when once again the great fact in the history of man, the most perfect unveiling of the Father through the Incarnation of the Word, is brought before us; and, starting from this, we are bidden to gaze into the future, and to realise the second more terrible, more glorious coming, when the veil of the Heavenly Temple shall be torn aside for ever, and the awful Presence shall be revealed to us in all His majesty, all His holiness, all His power, all His love, when we shall know, even as we are known—now on this day it is not unfitting that we should ask ourselves, how far our spiritual organs have grown used to the brightness of His presence, in what temper we have made the demand, 'Shew us the Father,' and whether we have deserved the rebuke, 'Have I been so long time with you, and yet hast thou not known Me?'

'Have I been so long time with you in the studies of this place, I, the Word of God, the expression of the Father's mind?' Have you busied yourselves with the manifold relations of number and space, and have the order, the simplicity of principles, the variety of results, the inexhaustible combinations, the infinite possibilities, chained and entranced you without striking one chord of religious awe, without inspiring one feeling of reverence towards the mind of the Eternal Word? Or has your time been spent on the investigation of external nature? Have you studied her in her grander developments, traced the motions of the heavenly bodies, the fluctuations of tides, the changes of seasons, followed the many divergent phenomena to the one, grand, comprehensive, all-pervading law, but have you stopped here? Has this law veiled, or has it revealed to you, the Eternal Word, of Whom it is the very sign-manual? Might it not be better, like the untutored barbarian, to see God in the clouds and to hear Him in the winds, than to refuse to see Him in the dynamic laws by which the clouds are shaped and reshaped, and to refuse to hear Him in the acoustic principles which give their voices to the winds? Or has your mind been directed to the investigation of more minute, but not less wonderful, processes of nature—the marvels of the vegetable world, for instance? What has 'a yellow primrose' been to you? A yellow primrose only, or something more? Yes, a little more; something of which you may count the stamens and the petals, something of which you may name the class and the genus and the species, of which you may investigate the structure and the functions and the geographical distribution. But has it, or has it not, been to you a revelation of the beauty, the order, the power, the love, of the Eternal Word? 'By Him all things were made, and without Him was not anything made that was made.' Has He been so long time with you, and yet have ye not known Him?

Or again; have you traced the intricate subtleties of language, examined its vocabulary and analysed its syntax, speculated on its origin, its development, its decay? And have you seen only adaptations of human organs, only processes of human thought?

Have you found no traces of the Father's presence here? Have you spent hour after hour on the literature of the two greatest nations of antiquity? And have you listened, as though only Greeks and Romans are speaking to you? Have you heard no echo of the Divine Word, sounding above and through the din of human voices; seen no impress of the Divine Mind —blurred and partial though it was—in the philosophic penetration of the one and the legal precision of the other? Have you pored over the long roll of human history—so much lengthened out for you in these later days by the discoveries of the ethnologer and the antiquarian—have you traced the successions of epochs, the divergences of races, mapped out their several provinces in the development of humanity, marked the lines of progress running through the ages, floated on the stream of knowledge and civilisation broadening slowly down? And has all this opened out no revelation of the Word, though the scroll is written over with His name within and without? He is the light and the life of men. These were records of continually enlarged life, of ever-increasing light. 'Has He been so long time with you, and have ye not known Him?'

I have spoken of the Word in nature, and the Word in history—of the Word in mathematical conceptions, and the Word in human speech. I have done so because to ourselves, as students, these applications of the text seem to appeal with peculiar force. It is here that we should learn to know the Word, and to see the Father. Yet once again I would not be mistaken. Neither philology, nor mathematics, nor nature, nor history will of themselves teach this lesson. But the Spirit will speak through these studies to the spiritually-minded: will quicken them with a higher life; will impart through them a revelation of God.

But to us, and to all alike, the Word of God has spoken in other and clearer tones. He became flesh, and He dwelt among us. He has lived on earth with us in the Gospels, and He lives still by His Spirit with us in the Church. He came to open the grave, to redeem us from sin, to sanctify our lives through His life. He came to quicken our natural yearnings after heaven, to enlighten our imperfect conceptions of deity. He came to bring home to our hearts the all-embracing love of God, Who sent His only-begotten Son to die for us, and to be a propitiation for our sins. He came to shew us, not the Omnipotent, not the Avenger, not the Judge, but the Father.

'And we have seen His glory'—seen it in the record of those three short years which speak to us in the pages of the Evangelists with a freshness and a force which no time can tarnish or decay; seen it in the long lapse of those eighteen centuries of Christian History, in which He has lived again in the lives of His saints, and died again in the sufferings of His heroes. Has He then been so long time with us, and yet have we not known Him? Do we still ask to be shewn the Father?

To have seen the Father—this is comfort, this is strength, this is joy, this is life. Have *we* seen Him —not *we* vaguely, but have *you* individually, have I individually? To those who have, such language will be felt to be no exaggeration. If only for a moment we have caught His shadow resting on our chamber wall, as He has passed by; if only in a fleeting glance we have arrested the glory streaming from the fringe of His mantle, then this one revelation has been to us a source of infinite satisfaction and strength —better far than months and years of our earthly, selfish, sinning life. When sorrow overclouds, when temptation assails, when sickness prostrates and death closes over us, this and this only—this sense of a Father's presence—can animate and sustain us, can give us energy to act and courage to bear.

Is it not worth while to strive hard for the attainment of this, worth while to pursue it with something more than the zeal of the athlete in pursuit of victory, or the student in pursuit of knowledge—with something of the desperate, pertinacious, absorbing passion, which the miser devotes to his hordes of gold. Without such earnestness it will not be attained. The loftiest crags are the hardest scaled. And this is the topmost crest of all, whence all the heights of human ambition are dwarfed into insignificance. It is not by listless aspirations, not by decent observance of religious forms, not by dutiful acquiescence in orthodox creeds, not by minute and painful criticism of the Scriptures, that the crown will be won: but by wrestling with the angel of God in prayer, and forcing a blessing from him; by cultivating to the utmost all your faculties of mind and soul, that you may offer to God a less unworthy gift; by sustained and rigorous discipline exerted over your passions, your desires, your sluggish neglects, your perverted activities; by the unreserved surrender of self to Him. So, and so only, may you hope that the Father will unveil Himself before you, will speak with you face to face, as a man speaketh with his friend.

For the young man, who is prepared to do this, who is ready to surrender not this or that desire only, but himself to God, a great work is in store—a work which may well fire the divinest ambition of youth, a work which is only possible at long intervals and in stirring times like the present. This is confessedly a great crisis in the history of the Church, in the history of the world—a crisis full of hopes, and full of fears. Of these hopes, these fears, you young men are the heirs. Our time is passing rapidly; our day is far spent. Something ere the end may perhaps yet be done—something, but very little. On you the future depends. When your call from God may come, what your commission from Him may be, I cannot tell. This is hidden in the depths of His counsels. But the preparation, the discipline, the self-surrender, must begin at once. Even now you must hasten to your Father's presence, and fall at your Father's feet. Do this, and wait patiently. The great work, it would seem, of your generation is to reconcile the present and the past. Study therefore the present in the light of the past, and the past in the light of the present; but study both in the light of the Divine Word. See in both, see in all things, the Father's presence. Take your commission directly from Him. Seek instruction directly from Him. He is the only infallible teacher. I know only too well, that he who speaks to you now has no claims from anything he has done, or anything he has suffered, to be heard on so lofty a theme; but I know this also, that, if he were allowed to indulge one hope only, it would be this; that a chance spark thrown off from his anvil should have burnt into the soul of some young man here present, and lie smouldering there, until hereafter it shall burst out into a flame, which shall rise ever higher and burn ever brighter, when he himself has passed away and is forgotten.

II.

THE SWORD OF THE WORD.

The word of God is quick, and powerful, and sharper than any two-edged sword, piercing even to the dividing asunder of soul and spirit, and of the joints and marrow, and is a discerner of the thoughts and intents of the heart. Neither is there any creature that is not manifest in His sight: but all things are naked and opened unto the eyes of Him with Whom we have to do.
HEBREWS iv. 12, 13.

Great S. Mary's Church, 21st Sunday after Trinity, 1870.

Do we want an illustration of the moral truth conveyed in these words? We shall not have to look far for an example. Of all the heroes in Jewish history, none would appear more enviable, as none was more successful or more famous, than David, the triumphant king, the sweet Psalmist of Israel, the man after God's own heart. We follow him step by step from the obscurity of his youth, till after many dangers and trials, through many vicissitudes, he has forced his way from the sheepfold to the throne. Seated there, he raises the power of his people, and the glory of the monarchy, to a height, which before him none could have foreseen, which after him none was destined to surpass. His success is now culminating. Everywhere respected, everywhere triumphant, honoured by his people and feared by his enemies, in all the consciousness of patriotic zeal, in all the plenitude of undisputed power, he might seem indeed to have attained such happiness as rarely falls to the lot of man. Moreover in his private life the same prosperity attends him. At this very moment he has accomplished a design which lies near to his heart; his well-laid plans have been carried out with secrecy and crowned with success; he is reaping the fruits of his stratagem. Who so proud, who so justly admired and envied as he? And yet at the very crisis of his triumph, in his mid-career of self-felicitation, the blow falls upon him; a sharp, chilling, piercing stroke from an unseen hand, which paralyses his whole being. And from what an unexpected quarter too does it fall! Not by famine or pestilence; not by defeat abroad or by revolution at home; not by loss of reputation, or loss of wealth, or loss of friends; not by disaster of any kind, as men reckon disasters, but by the agony of an awakened conscience. A simple child-like story uttered by a prophet's lips has wrought the miracle. The Israelite king feels in anguish of spirit the biting edge of a sudden remorse. His very success is his bitterest punishment. The overflowing cup of happiness is become a draught of deadliest poison. His sin has been brought home to him. Henceforth his life is all changed. He is no more hopeful, no more joyous, no more proud and self-reliant. Bowed down with shame and sorrow, he lies prostrate before the throne of grace. 'Against Thee only have I sinned.' 'Cast me not away from Thy presence, and take not Thy Holy Spirit from me.' 'O give me the comfort of Thy help again.' The echo of those few terrible words ever lingers in his ear, 'Thou art the man.'

Or again; pass from the Old Testament to the New. A very different scene awaits us here. From the captain of Israel we turn to the oppressor of Israel. A Roman governor is seated on his tribunal, protected by his guards and surrounded by the insignia of office. A man of unbridled passions and inhuman cruelty, he holds in his grasp the life and the property of all around him. Hated and feared by others, he knows no fear himself; he has no scruples, no misgivings of any kind. Before him stands a helpless prisoner, rude of speech, and mean in bodily presence, a poor invalid broken by cruel persecution and worn with distracting cares. He utters a few eager words on a strange topic. Do they seem like the dreams of a visionary or a fanatic? Certainly they take no account of the worldly schemes, the tangible advantages, the material pleasures, which absorb that ruler's thoughts. And yet, the bold reckless tyrant dares not listen, dares not face them. Paul reasons of righteousness, temperance and judgment to come; and Felix trembles.

I have set these two incidents side by side, because they are at once so like and so unlike the one to the other. In time, they are separated by the lapse of many centuries; and diverse forms of thought and usages of society and types of government have come and gone; and mighty nations have arisen and flourished and grown old and passed away meanwhile. In the principal actors also, the central figures in the two pictures, there is a direct contrast. The Israelite king, the devout servant of the one true God, has nothing in common with the reckless procurator, whose religion would have been idolatry, if he had had any religion at all; nothing in common at least, except his proneness to sin and his need of forgiveness. And, lastly, in the results the opposition is still more striking. David is overwhelmed with shame, and humbles himself before God: Felix stops his ears, and hardens his heart. Yet this broad gulf of time is spanned by one eternal power. Amidst all this diversity of circumstances, of persons, of consequences, there is one constant and abiding element; the unseen, but not unfelt, Witness and Judge, Who reveals and Who denounces sin. While all else changes, this alone remains unchangeable. For, though all flesh withereth like grass, and the glory of man falleth away, as the flower thereof, yet the Word of God endureth for ever. This mighty two-edged sword was the weapon wielded alike by Nathan and S. Paul. And, smitten thereby, David repented and Felix trembled.

The Word of God. Much controversy and much misapprehension have gathered about this simple phrase. From all controversy I hope to keep clear. The subject which I have chosen, the power of the Word of God in revealing sin, is deeper and higher and broader than any controverted topic of theology —deeper, for it penetrates into the inmost recesses of the human heart; higher, for it carries us before the throne of God; broader, for it allows no distinction between man and man. All alike fall within its scope.

But, if controversy should be avoided, misapprehension must be corrected. And to the true understanding of the text, the first step will be to discover what is meant by 'the Word of God.'

In the common language of our own time the Word of God is a synonym for the Scriptures, the Bible, the Record, the written Word. Men are so accustomed to this limitation, that they find it difficult to shake themselves loose from the force of habit. Yet in the Bible itself the expression is not so used; and even in our Church formularies, though the phrase frequently refers to the written Record, it is not limited to this.

Speaking generally, we may say that in the Bible itself the 'Word of God' is used as coextensive with Revelation in its widest sense. God's voice is God's declaration of Himself. Whensoever and howsoever He makes Himself known, there He speaks. Is it a precept, or a prediction, or a threat, or a promise? Is it a phenomenon of nature, or an act of grace? Is it an ordinary, or an extraordinary, exhibition of His power or His wisdom or His love? Does it speak to the eye by a written scroll, or does it speak to the ear through pulsations of air, or does it speak to the mind or the conscience with an impalpable, inaudible, motionless appeal? Whatever the subject, and whatever the mode of operation, the voice is still the same. In all these alike the Word of God is the agent or the agency, whereby He declares Himself.

Thus the application is comprehensive. Wherever Revelation is—Revelation natural or Revelation special—there is the Word of God. But, with this comprehensive bearing, the conception is two-fold. Sometimes the Word of God is the agent, sometimes the agency or the act. In other language it is sometimes personal, and sometimes impersonal.

1. The Word personal. The direct language of S. John, and the indirect language of S. Paul, apply the expression to a Divine Being, Who became man, and for one brief space lived on earth as man. He was before the worlds; through Him the worlds were created, and are governed. He is the expression of the Father's power, the Father's wisdom, the Father's love. He is the manifestation of God. His agency extends through all time, reaches back into the infinite past, and forward into the infinite future. Through Him is every revelation of God, whether natural or supernatural, whether in the world of sense or in the world of spirit. In His Incarnation, in His life and death and resurrection, the revelation of the Word culminates. Here its scattered rays are gathered into a focus. But it has begun countless ages before, and will continue countless ages after.

2. The Word impersonal. This is the most frequent, as it is the most obvious, use of the phrase. No longer the agent, but the operation or the agency, is denoted thereby. It is not now the speaker, but the speech, that is intended by the 'Word of God'—

the speech, but still in its comprehensive sense; the utterance which makes itself heard in nature and in history, the utterance which addresses itself to the hearts and consciences of men, not less than the utterance which communicates a special message to the prophet or the Apostle. 'By the Word of God the heavens were of old,' says S. Peter in one passage, and in another, 'Ye are born again by the Word of God.' 'His Word runneth very swiftly. He giveth snow like wool; He scattereth the hoarfrost like ashes...He sendeth out his Word, and melteth them;' so says the Psalmist, and in the very next verse he adds, 'He sheweth His Word unto Jacob, His statutes and His judgments unto Israel.' These two great facts which awed the soul of the modern philosopher—the starry heavens above, and the sense of moral responsibility within—what are they but the two-fold utterance of the Eternal Word of God?

In the text then the expression cannot be said of the written Word, for the usage of the Bible forbids this; neither can it be said of the personal Word, for the context does not encourage this meaning. It follows therefore that we adopt the third and only remaining sense, and understand it here of the operation or influence, which speaks to us from God and of God, which withdraws the veil of the material and sensible, which discloses to us the spiritual and unseen, alike in the phenomena of nature and the phenomena of grace—the same, of which it is written that, 'Man shall not live by bread alone, but by every Word that proceedeth out of the mouth of God.'

This Word, so comprehensive, so penetrating, has many functions. It instructs, it consoles, it stimulates, and encourages; but it also accuses and condemns. It addresses the understanding, the affections, the sympathies; but more especially it addresses the conscience. It is this last application to which the text refers. That man despises the Word of God and hardens his heart, as the people of old hardened their hearts in the wilderness, and brings down upon himself the like condemnation, and shuts himself out from the promised rest, who refuses to listen to the voice of right and truth, by whatsoever channel it reaches his ear, whether by the outspoken rebuke of a friend, or the angry taunt of a foe, or the inward workings of his heart, or the accidents of outward circumstances—if only he knows it to be God's voice —not less surely, not less fatally, than though it were uttered by an accredited messenger from Heaven, or appealed to him in the language, and through the facts, of Holy Scripture.

I spoke just now of the limited sense in which men commonly conceive and speak of the 'Word of God,' as not justified by the language of the Scriptures themselves. And yet this usage is only wrong, in so far as it is a limitation. I will not now discuss the more direct theological characteristics of the Bible, which vindicate its claim to this title as most legitimate and most true. I am rather concerned here with the moral power of the Word, for to this the text more directly points. And does not the written Record, the Bible, regarded in this aspect, satisfy the description most fully? It is living and active. Though the record of events transacted in bygone ages and in foreign lands, though the voice and the writing of men who have long since passed away, it is yet no dead letter, but a quick and a quickening spirit. It speaks still, as it has spoken ever, to the hearts and consciences of men; nay, it seems even to gain force and meaning by the lapse of ages. And it is a sharp two-edged sword also. It breaks the skin of social distinctions; it probes the conventional habits of a defective morality; it pierces to the inmost recesses of the soul; it severs, and it lays open.

When therefore we are discussing the language of the text, we should do well to bear in mind that though the Word of God and the Bible are not coextensive and so convertible terms, yet the Bible pre-eminently satisfies the requirements which are demanded of the Word of God in this definition.

And of all the tokens of Inspiration none is more striking, because none is more simple. It is the one evidence which makes no difference between mind and mind, which presupposes no previous special training, asks no laborious investigation or abstruse reasoning. The attestation of miracles requires careful weighing; the fulfilment of prophecy demands historical research; the marvellous oneness and continuity of the Scripture Revelation—manifesting the same increasing purpose throughout, yet manifesting it under various forms and in diverse ages (for the Bible is not a divine book, but a divine library, as it was truly called in times past)—this, which I venture to think the most weighty of all merely intellectual evidences, will not appear without much patient study and some concentration of thought. But here we are moving in a larger room, are breathing a free air. Here is neither Greek nor barbarian, learned nor unlearned, wisdom nor folly. Here is no parable of intricate meaning; 'Lo, now speakest Thou plainly, and utterest no proverb. Now we believe that Thou camest forth from God.'

We have seen what is implied by the 'Word of God,' as used in this passage. Let us turn now to the image, under which its power is described.

The victim bound with cords, helpless, prostrate on the altar; the sacrificial knife gleaming over him for a moment, then plunged into his neck; the convulsed limbs, the relaxing muscles, the quivering heart, the life ebbing out fast with the stream of his blood; the last, panting, throbbing gasp, and all is over. The victim is then separated limb from limb; the secret springs of his exuberant life are laid bare; the complex machinery of his active frame—bones, joints, muscles, arteries—all are seen. There is no concealment, no mystery now.

And is it an idle fancy, if we discern something more in the image than this? Metaphors borrowed from heathen sacrificial rites are familiar to us in S. Paul. The fragrant incense, which perfumes the sacrifice, is the diffusive benevolence of the Christian heart accompanying the surrender of self to God. The libation poured over the head of the victim is the Apostle's devotion of his own life to perfect the faith and self-sacrifice of his converts. The captives chained to the victor's car, the triumphal procession winding along the Sacred Way to the temple on the Capitoline Mount, represent the spirits of men subjugated by the power of the Gospel, the triumph of Christ Who ascends up on high and leads captivity captive. May there not then be a similar reference here to certain rites which accompanied a heathen sacrifice? May not the image refer to the inspection of the victim for the purpose of taking omens? The carcase is dissected; the vital parts are laid open; the abode of the passions and affections is exposed to scrutiny. Is the heart healthy and whole? Or is there in some hidden recess a dark plague-spot, the germ of an eating canker, some fatal propensity of pride or malice or indolence or sensuality or selfishness or self-seeking in some other form—unrevealed to those without, unfelt and almost unsuspected even by the victim himself, and yet a terrible omen foreboding ruin to himself, to his family, to the society in which he moves, to the Church of which he is a member, to the country which reckons him as a son. It is well that his heart should be torn open; well that the dark presage should be read in time, while yet all is not lost, while yet the fearful consequences may be averted. This revelation the Word of God will make: piercing, slaying, dissecting, like the sacrificial knife; but unlike it in this, that it heals most completely, where it wounds most deeply; and gives life there only, where first it has killed.

Such I suppose to be the force of the image in the text. But, whether this be so or not, it is clearly intended to suggest two main ideas, *revelation* and *chastisement*.

1. The Word of God is essentially a revelation of the secrets of the heart.

And here again we cannot fail to see how the Book, the Record, fulfils this condition of the Word of God. 'His words,' said one of the fathers speaking of S. Paul, 'are not words, but claps of thunder.' Might we not have added that they are lightning-flashes also, darting through the pitchy darkness, and revealing so suddenly, so unexpectedly, the deepest recesses of selfishness and sin in the human heart? This, which is true of S. Paul, true of the whole Bible, is pre-eminently true of the recorded sayings of Him, Who spake as never man spake, Who is Himself the very Word of God. I cannot attempt to describe this moral power of Holy Scripture in language. I dare not hope to add anything to the image in the text. The joints and the marrow of the human soul and spirit—the most complex interdependencies of passion and thought and purpose and action, and the vital centre and home of the moral life—both these the Word of God probes and severs and lays bare. It is just this dissecting power, this keen penetration of the Scriptural Record, which is its most wonderful moral feature. I have read in other books many wise and beautiful reflections on the relations of God and man, on life and death, on time and eternity, many lofty precepts and salutary rules for the guidance of human conduct, much of all kinds that instructs, improves, elevates. I have read such with deep thankfulness; and I believe that all light, whatever it may be, comes from the great Father of lights. But in no other book, unless its inspiration has been derived from this Book, do I find the same delicate discrimination between the real and the seeming in things moral, the same faculty of piercing through the crust of outward conduct and revealing the hidden springs of action, of stripping off all conventional disguises, of separating mixed motives with their contradictory elements of good and evil. This analysing, dissecting moral power is the logical attribute of the written Word.

2. But the metaphor in the text implies punishment also. The revelation which probes the intricate joints and the inmost marrow of the human soul and spirit, cannot do so without inflicting much bitter anguish. Take the case of one who, after living on for years in a dream-land of self-delusion, is awakened to a sense of his true character. His life perhaps has been one of uncheckered success throughout; he is happy in his friends and his family; he is in easy circumstances; he maintains a high reputation with the world. And meanwhile his outward prosperity

and calm have lulled him into a false security: he has come to survey his position and his character with infinite self-satisfaction. Then suddenly an unseen power flashes the truth upon him. He sees his own meanness, his selfishness, his hypocrisy and doubleness of heart. He is stabbed through and through with this new revelation. He is not worse now, he is very far better, than he was before. A converting, purifying influence, like a mighty rushing wind, has passed, or is passing, over him. Yet he was happy then, and now he is utterly wretched. Whence comes this difference? The world has not changed its opinion of him. It holds him upright and virtuous now, as it held him before. Good men seek his company and value his approbation still, as they did before. Is this new feeling then a mere phantom, a temporary mania? No: he knows that it is real; far more real than the haze of self-delusion, in which he has hitherto lived. And yet, if religion were not a true thing, if the distinction of good and evil were only a conventional distinction, a mere trick of education, the accumulated growth of ages, if morality were but a more imposing name for utility, then he would be right to fling these uncomfortable feelings aside, as idle fancies, unsubstantial ghosts, haunting his path and disturbing his peace. But this he dare not, he cannot do. He has felt the cutting edge of the Word of God. It has pierced to the dividing asunder of his inmost soul and spirit.

I have taken an instance of one suddenly awakened in conscience by the power of the Word. Let me exemplify this retributive power exercised under different circumstances and with different results, no longer in correction but in vengeance, no longer for repentance but for remorse. A man is indulging habitually in some sinful course, whether dishonesty or sensuality or some other form of vice. He plunges deeper and deeper in his guilt; he goes on and on, conscious whither he is led. He feels himself falling, falling downward, into the abyss: and his guilty heart keeps its own secret. He dares not reveal himself even to his closest and dearest friend. What account, I ask, is to be given of this state of mind, so truly described as the heaviest of all punishments, worse than the sword of Damocles, worse than the tortures of Phalaris, by the heathen moralist and poet, whose language, expressing as it does the deepest moral truth in the noblest form, the preacher speaking in the name of Christ need not apologize for adopting. It is certainly not the fear of worldly consequences: his guilt may be beyond the reach of punishment, perhaps even of detection. He may have no very distinct sense of right and wrong, and yet he feels somehow that he is despising the right and choosing the wrong. He may not confess God with his tongue or even in his heart, and yet he is conscious that an ever-widening gulf yawns between him and all that is noble and beautiful and good, that is to say, the mind of God; he is dimly conscious that he is alienating himself from God. This is the source of his hidden terror; God is witnessing within him, is denouncing him, is punishing him. He too has felt the cutting edge of the Word.

Are there any here, who have experienced that which I have attempted to describe; into whose soul this keen knife of the Word has pierced, healing with correction or slaying with remorse; who with David have repented, or with Felix have trembled? They will know that this sharp, painful shock cannot be wholly explained by the fear of detection or the dread of consequences; that beyond and above these lower influences a mightier hand wields the weapon. These may poison the barb, but they do not whet its point, nor direct its aim. In lower natures they will be more powerful. A brave man will despise them. It is only when that something which we call conscience whispers its tale in his ear, that the defiant eye is dropped, and the upraised arm sinks by his side, and he feels that the strength has gone out of him. His best ally, his inmost self, has turned against him; this it is, which unnerves, unmans him. 'Conscience doth make cowards of us all.'

And if conscience is not a mere function of utility, so neither is it an artificial growth of education. Would you object that in the child the distinction of right and wrong seems merged in the idea of obedience or disobedience to external authority; that with the savage the conception of morality appears hardly to rise above the desire of appeasing, or the fear of offending, his fetich? What then: would you go to the child for a clear idea of syllogistic reasoning? To the savage for an adequate definition of scientific induction? And if you would not, then why should you do in the one case, what you would not do in the other? Education *does* develope; experience *does* ripen. This is true of the moral consciousness, as it is true of the intellectual reason. But neither education, nor experience, can create. The germ, the faculty, is there, there in the child and in the savage, as in the full-grown civilized man, bound up, we know not how, with the phenomena of our physical nature, influenced by them and influencing them in turn, but heaven-descended and heaven-implanted.

'Conscience doth make cowards of us all.' It is said, and said truly. But, if this be all, then its work is imperfect, is worse than useless. 'Sin revived and I died,' says S. Paul. But this is only a first stage. Death cannot be the rule of life. 'God did not give us the spirit of cowardice, but of power and of love and of a sound mind.'

Conscience makes cowards of us; but conscience makes saints and heroes also; *saints*, for the perfect harmony, perfect guilelessness, perfect gentleness of character which we call saintliness, will only come to those who are ever sensitive to the most subdued tones of the still small voice, which speaks to us alike in the silence of the closet and the turmoil of the streets: *heroes*, for though there be heroes many, as the world counts heroes, whom ambition or vainglory or self-seeking have made bold and defiant, yet the true hero, the man (as he was painted of old) who is content to live a life of obloquy and die a death of shame, who strives to be just, more than to be called just—as Christians let us add also, to be pure, more than to be called pure—he can only be created by the consciousness of this Higher Presence, can only be sustained by the monitions of this Divine Witness within him. 'His Word was in my heart as a burning fire.'

Youth and early manhood are the seed-time of the conscience, not less but even more than of the intellect. God's law, which ordains that a man's heart shall harden itself by neglect and selfishness and disobedience, till one by one each avenue is closed to His Spirit, and a thick, impervious crust encases the whole—this law, however mysterious as a dispensation, is a plain stubborn fact which daily experience confirms. I do not doubt that with you, young men—not with a few but with many—personal consciousness has winged the arrow and driven the image in the text home to your hearts. At some time or other, in one or more of many ways, the sword has pierced your soul; the Word of God, witnessing in you and against you, has found its way to the vital parts. It has done so, and it will do so again. But this will not last for ever. Instead of the sharp, short pang, which wounds only to heal, a moral numbness, a paralysis ending but in death may creep on at last. Do not therefore resist; do not sear the wound. If you entertain the high ambition, not only to pass through the world in respectability and comfort, not only to achieve a success more or less brilliant, but to do and to suffer, above all to be that which God wills for you, then this His Word speaking through your conscience is your real and only teacher. Honesty and truthfulness are the elements of morality; humility and reverence and purity are its head and crown. For the former the restraints of law and convention, the demands and the sympathies of social life may do not a little; for the latter they will effect almost nothing. These must grow from within. This inward monitor, and this alone, can create and sustain them.

Therefore do not shield yourselves against the cutting double-edge of this Sword of God. Bear the pain, that you may find the cure. 'He hath torn, and He will heal us; He hath smitten, and He will bind us up.' Is it not significant, that in the words immediately following on the text—as the sequel and the counterpart to this description of the piercing, revealing, slaying Word of God—we are led at once into the presence of our great High Priest in the heavens, Who is 'touched with a feeling of our infirmities,' being tempted like us, though unlike us sinless, and bidden to 'come boldly unto the throne of grace, that we may obtain mercy, and find grace to help in time of need.'

III.

THE HEAD AND THE BODY.

That we may grow up into Him in all things, Which is the head, even Christ; from Whom the whole body fitly joined together and compacted by that which every joint supplieth, according to the effectual working in the measure of every part, maketh increase of the body unto the edifying of itself in love.

EPHESIANS iv. 15, 16.

Great S. Mary's Church, 22nd Sunday after Trinity, 1870.

MY text last Sunday appealed to the secret experience of the individual heart: my text to-day refers to the mutual relations and interdependencies of a vast and varied society. The theme then was necessarily concentrative; the theme now will be essentially diffusive.

I introduced the text as taken from the Epistle to the Ephesians. At the very outset this statement needs amendment; for, if true, it is only partially true.

We know now that the Epistle, which we are accustomed so to designate, was addressed to a much wider circle of readers. As S. Peter later writes to the strangers scattered throughout several districts in Asia Minor, as S. John later still addresses the Divine message to the principal Churches of the Roman province called Asia, so (there is good reason to think) the destination of S. Paul's letter was not Ephesus only, the metropolis of the region, but all the Christian communities established in the several populous centres—perhaps throughout the province, perhaps extending over a still wider area. This result we may consider to be established by recent investigation and criticism. In the copies used by more than one of the ancient fathers, the words 'in Ephesus' were absent from the opening verse. They are wanting in the two oldest MSS. which time has spared to us. Plainly these copies were derived from an archetype, in which a blank had been left for the name of the Church and had never been filled in. Another still more ancient writer called this the Epistle to the Laodiceans. Clearly he fell in with a copy addressed, not to Ephesus, but to Laodicea. And, if it be asked, how the common title prevailed, how the Church came to receive this as an Epistle to the Ephesians, the answer is simple. From Ephesus, the most populous city and the most important Church, the political and ecclesiastical metropolis of the region, the most numerous copies would be disseminated; and as some definite title was necessary, Ephesus, occupying this vantage ground, usurped the room and displaced the name of the other Churches in the heading of the Epistle.

The Epistle was an encyclical, a catholic Epistle. This hypothesis, as it is demanded by external testimony, is necessary also to explain the internal character of the letter. Critics had observed that there was an entire absence of all personal and local allusions in it, and they had objected that in a communication written to a Church, with which the Apostle was on the closest and most affectionate terms, in which he had resided three whole years, labouring night and day, this silence was most strange and inexplicable. They were therefore disposed to question the Apostolic authorship. Certainly, if it had been addressed to the individual Church of Ephesus, I do not know how we could explain the absence of all marks of individuality, or what answer could be given to the objection founded thereupon. But criticism has solved the difficulties, which itself created. It has pulled down, only to build up on a broader and stronger basis. It has vindicated the

Epistle to S. Paul, but it has denied the claims of Ephesus as the exclusive destination.

Copies then of this circular letter were entrusted to the bearer, Tychicus, who (as you will remember) is charged in the letter itself to deliver orally the special messages, the special information, which S. Paul desired to communicate to each Church severally. Thus one copy would be left at Ephesus, another at Sardis, a third at Thyatira, a fourth at Laodicea, and so with the remaining Churches to which the several transcripts were addressed. Laodicea was the chief city of the district in which the smaller town of Colossæ was situated. The Epistle to the Colossians was despatched at the same time, and by the same messenger, as this circular letter. Hence the Colossians are charged to get and read the copy which was sent to the neighbouring Laodicea. If there was any obscurity in the terms of this brief message, Tychicus, the bearer of both letters, was at hand to clear it up.

This is perhaps one of the most instructive results of Biblical criticism. But I should not have dwelt so long upon the subject merely for the sake of its critical interest. In all S. Paul's Epistles the subject-matter is determined by the destination. This is especially the case with the letter before us. Its encyclical character explains its main theme—the

Church as one, and yet manifold; one, as united in Christ; manifold, as comprising various members, various functions.

The Churches, to which the letter was addressed, had their several capacities, their distinct interests, their special advantages and their special temptations. The respective messages addressed in the Apocalypse to the Seven Churches enable us to appreciate the different tempers and conditions of these several communities. Side by side were the Church of Smyrna which in spite of poverty was rich, and the Church of Laodicea which boasting of its wealth was miserably poor; side by side, the Church of Ephesus which had left its first love, and the Church of Thyatira whose last works were more than the first; side by side, the Church of Pergamos where prevailed the doctrine of Balaam, the excess of Gentile sensuality, and the Church of Philadelphia where was established the synagogue of Satan, the excess of Jewish formalism.

Addressing these various communities, the Apostle cannot occupy himself with the refutation of individual errors, with the remedy of individual needs. Rather he seeks for some one grand comprehensive theme, which shall correspond to the comprehensive destination of the Epistle. This theme he finds in the idea of the Church as embracing all the Churches, the ideal community regarded as one harmonious whole, but comprising diverse branches, diverse offices, diverse members. Starting from the phenomenon of variety, he arrives at the idea of unity. He seeks the centre of union, the principle of cohesion, in Christ the Head. They all are one body, animated by one spirit; they all acknowledge one faith, into which they have been admitted by one baptism; they all are united in the one Lord, and through Him draw near to the one God and Father of all, Who is above all, and through all, and in all.

This then—the relation of the many to the One, of the Christians and the Churches to Christ and to one another through Christ—is the main theme of the Epistle. In one form or another it will be discerned running through paragraph after paragraph, inspiring alike the doctrinal statements and the practical injunctions; and it culminates in the words of the text.

Under three images especially this relation is developed.

1. The Church is the Bride; Christ is the Bridegroom. Here a special aspect of this connexion is figured. The purity of love, the singleness of devotion, the perfection of obedience, the entire oneness of interests and aims—these are the features especially brought out. 'They twain shall be one flesh.' 'This

is a great mystery.' 'I speak concerning Christ and the Church.'

2. The Church is a Temple; Christ the Chief Corner-Stone. This again, though a very expressive image, is yet partial. The compactness, the coherence, are prominent in it. The succession of layers, the stratification of the edifice, is also significant. And lastly, the object of the erection, the indwelling of the Spirit, finds its proper place.

3. But far more expressive and more full is the third and remaining image, the image of the text. Christ is the Head; the Church is the Body; each individual is a member, a limb, of the whole. This image supplies what was deficient in the last, the idea of mobility, vigorous life, diffused through the whole from one central, guiding, inspiring, vivifying power, the idea of an internal principle of growth, the idea of infinite variety of conditions, functions, needs, in the several parts, and combined with this the idea of the closest sympathy and interdependency, so that each is sensitive to the action of the other, and each necessary to the well-being of the whole.

The language of the text is not free from exceptional difficulties. Of these, however, I need not speak. They do not affect the significance of the image, either as a whole or in its several parts; and therefore they may well be neglected.

Setting aside these minor points as unimportant, we may paraphrase the passage thus.

The Church of Christ is one colossal being, a single body animated by a single soul. It has not yet attained its maturity; its powers are still undeveloped; its growth still imperfect; it has hardly yet passed its infancy. But grow it will, and grow it must, for growth is the law of its being. And this growth can only be attained in one way. Connexion with the Head is the indispensable condition; obedience to the Head the inseparable accompaniment. As in the human body there is an almost infinite variety of parts—bones, muscles, veins, arteries, nerves; so likewise in the Church you have the same manifold combination of diverse elements—different individuals, different capacities, different communions, different nationalities. Each one of these supplies some distinct want, performs some distinct office, which is necessary to the well-being of the whole. We speak of a good constitution. If a man has a good constitution, we say, he will rally after this or that attack, he will survive this or that wound. What is implied by this? That the setting together of the different parts, which combine to form the body, is harmonious; that the machinery of the human frame, as a whole, works well, works without any jarring or any entanglement; that not only each part has its proper development, but that the relative adjustment of the parts is true; that they preserve their separate independence, and yet respect their mutual interdependence. In like manner the different branches, functions, capacities in the Church work separately, but work for and into each other. They are knit together in one compact whole. Nay, more than this. They cannot exist separately. It is this very connexion that preserves their vitality. It is by adaptation and contact with the neighbouring parts, and through these with the whole body, that each receives that degree and that kind of nutriment which is necessary to sustain it.

But the centre of this cohesion, this correlation, this cooperation, is the Head. Here resides the power which controls, commands, animates, harmonizes the whole. Through orders transmitted from this central government, each part receives its directions, and in obedience thereto fulfils its work. Each acts singly; each performs its own task. The eye sees, and the feet walk, and the hands handle; and, so far as regards the particular action of each, there is no direct connexion between them. It is just because there is a centre of union, to which each severally refers, that the functions of all are directed to some one definite end, and that an adequate result is achieved.

Thus composed, thus united, thus controlled, the body grows—grows towards its ideal limit, the full moral stature, the perfect standard, of which the Person and the Life of Christ are the measure; while, throughout, the pervading element in which it moves, which it breathes, from which it derives sustentation and strength, is love.

This image of the Head and the Body must have had a speaking significance to the Apostle's contemporaries. To ourselves it presents itself with even greater vividness and force, in the light of later discoveries. The two main points in this relation are summed up in the two prepositions used to describe it in the text—'into Him' and 'from Him.' There is a concentrative energy tending towards the Head; and there is a diffusive energy spreading from the Head.

The head, the brain, is the initiative centre of our actions; and it is also the receptive centre of our sensations. From it all the various motions of the body are originated; and to it the manifold impressions of the senses are communicated. By two sets of nerves, as by two sets of telegraphic wires, this twofold communication with the head, as the central office, the seat of government in the human frame, is maintained. By the one set, the brain, the thinking, planning, originating power, transmits its orders to the furthest member; the order is received; the muscle contracts; the joint is moved; and the hand holds, or the foot walks. By the other set, the reverse process is carried on; the grasp which presses the hand, the rays which strike the eye, the pulsations which beat on the ear, all these are transmitted to the centre, and the corresponding sensation is thereby and there produced.

Such also is the relation of Christ to the Church. His control guiding the various members, and His sympathy feeling with the various members—these are the functions which this image brings clearly out.

1. There is the *controlling power*. The direction, the influence, the illuminating, guiding energy of the Eternal Word of God, is infinitely varied and extends throughout mankind. Of this however I do not intend to speak, though in these Epistles of S. Paul it assumes a prominent place. But it is rather the more definite, concentrated form of this control, which the same Word exerts, as the Incarnate Christ, not as the Head only of Universal Nature, but as the Head of the Church specially, that we are led by the text to consider. His teaching, His example, His Incarnation and Passion are the manifestation of the Father's love, His Resurrection is the manifestation of the Father's power—these are the outward agency;

the Spirit, Which the Father sendeth in His name—this is the invisible medium, through which He controls and enlightens and directs His Church. Thus He communicates the Almighty Will to us. Not veiling but revealing the Father, not interposing between man and God, but reflecting God to man, He acts upon the Church. And it is just according as we, the individual members of His Body, preserve our communication with Him; according as (in the language of the parallel passage in the Epistle to the Colossians) we 'hold fast the Head,' that is, according as our life is conformed to His life, our spirit interpenetrated with His Spirit, our being incorporated in His Being, that His orders are duly received, prompt, healthy, vigorous action ensues, and the will of the Father is done. The joint may be dislocated by worldly indulgence and distraction; or the limb may be paralysed by spiritual carelessness. If so, there will be no response, or no adequate response, to the message transmitted. But if the communication is intact, then, by a necessary spiritual law, action must follow, obedience must be complete.

2. But, secondly, the *sympathetic office* of Christ is suggested by the image. As the natural body, so also the spiritual body has its system of nerves, which communicate the sensations of its lowest, most distant, members to the Head. This entire sympathy of

Christ is no after-thought of the Apostle's, no idle fancy of an overwrought imagination, or outgrowth of unrestrained metaphor. The 'crucifying of the Son of God afresh' has its parallel in Christ's own declarations. No language of S. Paul or of the Epistle to the Hebrews can express this truth more strongly than His own words—recorded (be it observed) not in this instance by S. John, but by the other Evangelists— 'Inasmuch as ye did it unto one of the least of these My brethren, ye did it unto Me.' 'Inasmuch as ye did it not unto one of the least of these, ye did it not unto Me.' With the humblest member of His body He suffers: with the humblest member also He rejoices.

The image of the human body, as representing a society with its many members and various functions, was not new. The newness consisted in the significance of the Head. This was necessarily so; for the revelation of the Person, Who was the Head, was new. In the familiar apologue, addressed to the Roman crowd, the 'kingly-crowned head,' though it may be mentioned, means nothing, adds nothing, to the moral of the story. And if the popular application was defective, the philosophic was equally so. For the Stoic too spoke of society, of the world, of the universe, as one vast body of which individual parts and individual men were members. He went so far as to imagine it animated by one soul. But the image was vague, inarticulate, fruitless. It made no appeal to the experience, none to the heart, none to the consciences of men. He said nothing, could say nothing, of the Head. The body was to him a huge, headless, shapeless trunk, living a sort of unconscious, vegetable life, hanging together by a loose, uncertain, inappreciable bond.

This defect, which attended the popular and the philosophical application alike, was first supplied by the teaching of the Apostles, as it first became possible by the revelation of the Gospel. The Son of Man, the Pattern and Ideal of humanity, the Chief of His race, the Son of God, the Image of the Father, the Incarnation of the Divine Word—He Who centred in Himself both natures, He and He only could claim this place. From Him all the members must draw their inspiration, their strength; to Him all the members must direct their actions, must render their account. To hold fast to Him, to grow into Him, this has been the secret of the highest life. Above all the jarring conflicts of creeds, amid all the distracting forms of Church polity, this presence, this consciousness, this intimate relation, has been the one constant, guiding, inspiring, strengthening, renovating energy. And, in and by His name, lives of unsullied saintliness have been lived, and works of transcendent heroism wrought, by men in different ages, of different Churches, in different lands; because through Him they all alike have grown into a more perfect knowledge of the truth and the perfections of the Eternal Father.

But the image in the text speaks especially of the diversity resulting in unity. It tells of a harmony which comes from the due performance by each several member of its special function, the energetic working of every part in its proper measure or relation—for so it would seem we should translate the words κατ' ἐνέργειαν ἐν μέτρῳ ἑνὸς ἑκάστου μέρους.

There is an ideal of the Church, which confuses unity with uniformity, which would force every section and every individual into the same mould, which would exact of every age the same work, and is disappointed in not finding what it exacts. This is not the Apostle's conception. Uniformity would be fatal to the higher harmony which he requires. The unvaried repetition of the same function would be comparatively barren. The richness and the fulness of the result depend on the countless variety of the energies thus working together. 'All the members have not the same office.' 'If they were all one member, where were the body?'

The examples, which the Apostle selects, are necessarily limited to the experience of the infant

Church; but the principle is of the widest application. To us, who can look back on a history of eighteen centuries, the image will speak with much fuller significance than to S. Paul's immediate hearers. We may observe, how each great subdivision of the human race in turn has contributed its special work to the building of the Church; how the intellectual subtlety of the Greek was instrumental in drawing up her creeds and elucidating her doctrines; how the instinct of organization and the respect for order in the Latin moulded and strengthened her political and social life; how the self-devoting enthusiasm of the Celt gave the immediate impulse to her greatest missionary labours; how the truthfulness and stedfastness of the Teuton reformed her corruptions and brought her into harmony with the intellectual and the social acquisitions of a more enlightened age. We might turn from Churches to individuals; and we might point out, how an Origen, an Athanasius, a Benedict of Nursia, a Francis of Assisi, a Luther, each in his generation by his special gift, his special energy, introduced a distinct element, did a distinct work in the Church. Nay, we might even appeal to sects, and shew that however one-sided, however erroneous, each nevertheless has contributed something, has brought into prominence some neglected or half-forgotten aspect of truth. In this and diverse ways we might illustrate the Apostle's image of 'the whole body fitly joined together and compacted by that which every joint supplieth.'

But the task would be long. And the time which remains will be better employed in directing the lesson of the image to ourselves.

We here are all members of one body, of a whole compacted of various parts, are members of an University.

An University may be regarded as a Church within a Church, a Church viewed especially from its intellectual side. The name, and the thing alike, imply the same idea as the image of the text—multiplicity and unity—not manifoldness only, but manifoldness resulting in harmony and in oneness.

(1) This is an University of sciences. Such is the original idea of the term. It aims, or it should aim, at teaching every branch of knowledge. Each of us selects, or should select, his own study or studies, as the object of all the energies and powers of his mind. If I venture to urge the lesson of the text in connexion herewith, it is because I feel that these our studies will be pursued most truthfully and most profitably in the spirit there recommended, and that the consecration of the intellect to God thus attained is the highest achievement of man. And by pursuing our studies in the spirit of this image I mean

two things; first, that each individually should follow his own pursuit with all his might; and secondly, that there should be no jealousy, no impatience, no contempt, of the studies of others.

I do not think either caution unneeded at the present time. As the sphere of human knowledge enlarges, it becomes more and more necessary, that each should make choice of his pursuit and concentrate himself on this. He should make his choice, and he should believe in his work. No branch of study is contemptible, none is fruitless. Each has its place, each conduces to the well-being of the whole. 'Nay, much more those members of the body, which seem to be more feeble, are necessary.' Not to make a brilliant display, not to satisfy an appetite for diffusive reading, not to dissipate our intellectual energies, but to achieve something, to add something —however little—to the store of human knowledge— this should be the aim of all.

But this caution is not complete without the other. It is not only necessary that we should believe in our own work, but also that we should leave room for the work of others. This conflict between the old studies and the new, between theologians and men of science, between the investigation of the faculties of mind and the investigation of the phenomena of nature, should have no place with us. There is need of all; there is room for all; there must be no jealousy or depreciation of any, for none can be spared. Reason tells us, as S. Paul tells us, that 'if one member suffer, all the members suffer with it.' Reason shews us, as S. Paul shews us, a more excellent way, a comprehensive charity in the intellectual as in the social community, which 'beareth all things, believeth all things.' Thus bearing and thus believing, content 'to labour and to wait,' we shall look forward in faith to the time when the unity to which science, not less than religion, points, shall be attained, when the manifold cords of human knowledge shall be knotted in one, and attached to the throne of Heaven.

(2) But this is not only an University of studies; it is also an University of men. We bring to this place our different trainings, different experiences, different capacities. We each contribute something, and we receive much in turn. Here, if anywhere, the lesson of the text is exhibited in daily life, written in large characters that he may run that reads. This our body is large enough to afford the requisite variety, and small enough to be sensitive throughout to the healthy or unhealthy working of each individual part. A good example is more immediately felt here than elsewhere; a bad example spreads with fatal rapidity. Here, if anywhere, the moral interdependence of the members is close and sympathetic.

Here no man can evade responsibility, no man can live to himself. If he is not a centre of light and health, he must become a centre of darkness and disease. He may count many a habit innocent, because he does not trace any immediate evil consequences to his own character. Could he hold it so, if he saw its effect on others? A lavish personal expenditure, for instance, seems to him very allowable, if it does not exceed his means; but extravagance in one calls forth extravagance in others, and the disease thus feeds itself, and his expensive tastes beget a fashion of expenditure which may prove the ruin of many a poorer man, both body and soul. Or he is reckless in his language, talks lightly of moral obligations, talks scoffingly of religious truths or religious men. To himself this does not mean much; it is a random shaft shot idly into the air; but it has lodged in another's breast, has poisoned his thoughts, has mortally wounded his moral nature. 'I say unto you, that every idle word that men shall speak, they shall give account thereof in the day of judgment.'

It is enough, more than enough, to answer for our own ill deeds. It will be an intolerable, crushing load, if we have to bear also the burden of another's sins. The curse of one thus misled, thus degraded, thus lost by our carelessness, might well 'drag to hell a spirit from on high.' Remember this now. Resolve thus much at least, that through your influence, your example, no member of the body shall suffer. And to render this your resolution effectual, you will not forget that one safe way, and one only, is open ; that, if you would do your duty to the members, you— each one of you individually,—must preserve healthy, vigorous, intimate connexion with the Divine Head. So only will you do your several parts. So only will harmonious action ensue. So only will the whole body grow ever more and more to the edifying of itself in love.

IV.

THE WRATH OF THE LAMB.

The wrath of the Lamb.
REVELATION vi. 16.

Great S. Mary's Church, 20th Sunday after Trinity, 1873.

THIS title—the Lamb, the Lamb of God—as applied to our Lord, is found only in the Gospel and the Apocalypse of S. John. Like the designation of the 'Word of God,' or the image of the Shechinah, the tabernacle, the glory abiding among men, it is a distinguishing feature which connects these two books, and points to the identification of the disciple of love with the eagle-eyed seer of Patmos. Elsewhere indeed the image is indirectly suggested. But, as a proper name, an absolute and indefeasible title, it occurs in these two books alone.

And, as it links the Gospel with the Apocalypse,

so does it also connect the earliest days of Christ's dispensation with the latest. It is heard first on the lips of the forerunner alone, when the ministry on earth is now to begin; it is echoed last by ten thousand times ten thousand voices of the redeemed, when the ministry in heaven has drawn to a close. Its earlier utterance is the prelude to a life of toil and sorrow and shame and cruel agony: 'Behold, the Lamb of God, that taketh on Him the sins of the world.' Its later utterance is the final pæan of victory over death and hell, the triumphant hallelujah of glorified myriads swelled by the universal chorus of heaven and earth and sea, and prolonged into the echoes of eternity; 'Worthy is the Lamb that was slain.' 'Blessing and honour and glory and power be unto Him that sitteth upon the throne, and unto the Lamb for ever and ever.'

In the Gospel, however, the name, twice repeated on one single occasion, is never heard again. In the Apocalypse it is reiterated not far short of thirty times. Every other title of dignity seems to be swallowed up in this. No attribution of strength, and no panegyric of victory, and no outpouring of thanksgiving, and no ascription of praise seems to be complete, unless the homage is offered to the Lamb, the Lamb that was slain.

Some here will recall a famous work of early

Flemish art, in which the brothers Van Eyck have attempted to represent the luxuriant imagery of this Apocalyptic vision. All the lines in the picture converge towards a common centre. All the groups are arranged with reference to this one point. Martyrs, virgins, priests, prophets, hermits, pilgrims, holy warriors, righteous judges, kneeling or standing, on foot or on horseback, at rest or in motion—all are gathered or gathering about one prominent figure. On it each eye is gazing, and towards it each footstep moves. These various groups of redeemed and glorified saints stud the outer parts of the picture. More central than these is an inner circle of winged angels, some bearing the instruments of the Passion, some swinging censers, but all with faces upturned towards this one point, all kneeling in adoration of this one figure. Highest of all and directly above it is One of stately mien and majestic visage, seated on a throne, His head crowned with a tiara, His hand raised in the attitude of benediction. It is the Eternal Father Himself, Whom with the unconscious irreverence of his age, which striving to communicate the incommunicable ended only in limiting the illimitable, the artist has represented in a human form. At His feet is a richly jewelled crown ready, it would seem, to descend and encircle the brow of the figure beneath. Immediately below, still hovering over this central figure, is a dove with outstretched wings, the symbol of the Spirit, darting forth rays of light and encircled in clouds of glory. Lowest of all, beneath the feet of the saintly groups and right under the central figure itself, was once a representation of the souls in agony. This part of the picture is now effaced; but we may well imagine that the motive was suggested by the words of the text; that the centre of attraction to the redeemed was a centre of repulsion to the lost; that with cowering limbs and averted eyes they shunned the glory of the Adorable One; that in their mien, in their every gesture and look, they seemed to say to the mountains, 'Cover us,' and to the hills, 'Fall on us.'

And this one figure, which thus gathers into itself the glory of the whole picture; this centre, towards which all things gravitate by an irresistible force; this common object of adoration, to which heaven and earth alike yield homage—what is it? Surely here the painter will lavish all the treasures of his art, and tax all the resources of his brain, to produce some conception, which in elevation of ideal and splendour of colouring, in dignity and pathos and beauty and strength, shall be worthy of its position. But what do we find? We look to this central figure, and our feeling is one of blank disappointment. The object of adoration here is not the calm and stately form, so awful and yet so loving, with arms outstretched to bless and shewing the wounded palms, like the glorified Saviour of Angelico; nor the Crucified One, nailed still to the Cross, but transferred from earth to heaven, and held up in the arms of the Everlasting Father for awe-stricken myriads to adore, as this same subject is treated by Dürer, another great master. There is no power, no beauty, no elevation in the conception here. The artist has fallen into a naked, painful literalism. He seems determined that the adoration of the Lamb shall be the adoration of a lamb; and a lamb he has given us. There is an incongruity, a perversity, a paradox, a bathos, in this treatment which we can hardly explain and cannot forgive.

Yet this literalism, this bathos of treatment, however faulty in itself, does emphasize a leading characteristic of the Apocalyptic vision. The artistic paradox of the painter answers to the moral paradox of the seer. S. John plainly dwells upon this title with affectionate fondness, just because it is incongruous. Nay, he seems bent on enhancing the incongruity by all the accessories which he can gather about it, welcoming every paradox of language and every inversion of metaphor which will give point to his lesson. Though a lamb, it is the shepherd of the flock, leading the sheep to springs of living water and followed by them, wheresoever it goes (vii. 17, xiv. 4). Though a slain lamb, it has power over the Book of Life (xiii. 8). Though its blood is crimson, it has a cleansing, bleaching efficacy, washing white the robes of the redeemed (vii. 14). And altogether, this feeblest, most timid, most gentle, most helpless creature, is an emblem of strength, of power, of victory. Once indeed the Apocalyptic seer stumbles on an image more akin (we might have thought) to the ideas which he wishes to convey— 'Behold, the Lion of the tribe of Judah.' Here was a magnificent image, recommended alike by its prophetic prestige, by its historic relations, and by its intrinsic propriety. The monarch of the forest, springing on his prey, would suggest just those conceptions of sovereignty and vengeance and might, with which he would desire to invest the Person of the glorified Lord. Yet it is dropped at once and for ever; and the image of the Lamb replaces it, never again to be relinquished. The mode of transition too is remarkable. 'One of the elders said unto me... Behold, the Lion of the tribe of Judah...And I beheld, and, lo...a Lamb as it had been slain.' This novel contradiction lies at the root of the Gospel. The life of Christ was from first to last a paradox. His weakness was power; His shame was honour; His death was victory. The life of the Church is a paradox also. Among the most distinguished warriors have been the feeble and the foolish and the despised of the world. Again and again her strength has been made perfect in weakness; again and again the things, that are not, have been chosen to confound the things, that are. Thus the lamb, not the lion, is the true symbol of our faith. This is plainly the leading idea in the Apocalypse. Whatever of greatness and whatever of power the seer would ascribe to his risen Lord finds its reason, its justification, its fulfilment in this one title. Is it victorious might? 'These shall make war with the Lamb, and the Lamb shall overcome them.' Is it divine illumination? 'The glory of God did lighten it, and the Lamb is the light thereof.' Is it adoration and worship? 'Worthy is the Lamb that was slain to receive power, and riches, and wisdom, and strength, and honour, and glory, and blessing.' Lastly; is it vengeance? 'Hide us...from the wrath of the Lamb; for the great day of His wrath is come.'

Here is the climax of the paradox. It is not the wrath of the Lion, but the wrath of the Lamb, which is so terrible in the seer's vision. In its innocence, in its meekness, in its tenderness, this gentlest of all creatures is endowed with a capacity of retribution, which is denied to the monarch of the forest with all his fierceness and all his might. The old riddle is inverted; and out of sweetness comes forth strength. How then must we read it?

The punishment of the wicked was a theme of terrible fascination with the painters of an earlier age. They taxed all the fertility of a morbid fancy to paint the physical tortures of lost souls. What did they hope to gain by this hideous play of the imagination? Did they think to frighten the vulgar into well-doing? Nay; might not the very familiarity with such horrible conceptions stimulate those passions which they sought to check; just as the public execution of a criminal is said to be a fruitful source of fresh crime? Or did they imagine that they had Scriptural authority for these pictures, even as symbolic imagery? Nay; the strange thing is, that though their representations of heaven are largely taken from the Apocalypse, their representations of hell are the creations of their own brain. It is a remarkable, and it is surely a significant fact, that while the bliss of the redeemed is painted by the Apocalyptic seer with all the varied imagery which an inspired imagination can command, though the picture is repeated again and again with ever-increasing energy of delineation, yet there is no corresponding description of the lost. Once or twice the familiar symbol of the fiery lake is introduced; but it is briefly dismissed again. The Apostle would appeal to spiritual aspirations, rather than to physical terrors. Fear may deter; but fear cannot educate. Love only is the educator of the soul. Hence for the most part a thick veil is drawn over the fate of the lost, which later ages attempted rudely, but vainly, to pluck away. Here and there indeed a glimpse is accorded, only to suggest a wholly different order of ideas. 'Every eye shall see Him, even they which pierced Him.' 'Hide us from the face of Him that sitteth on the throne, and from the wrath of the Lamb.'

It is not physical agony, if we read the interpretation aright; it is the beauty of holiness, it is the splendour of purity, it is the majesty of truth, it is the tenderness of love, which shall be the chief instrument of retribution. It is the blessing spurned, and the opportunity lost, which shall start up from the oblivion of the past, and confront us as God's angel of vengeance. It is the glory and the goodness, in which we yearn to slake our burning thirst, and lo! the cup is dashed away from our lips. What was it that wrung from those foolish ones in the parable, the mournful hopeless cry, 'Lord, Lord, open to us?' Not certainly the howling of wild beasts, nor dread of robbers, nor deadly night-chill, nor menacing storm. As for all these, they had slept securely hitherto, and might sleep on again. It was the awakening and finding that the door was closed, and they were in the darkness without. There was the light streaming through the casement, and the shadow of the bridegroom thrown on the chamber wall—the light which they might not share, and the bridegroom whom they might not greet. Aye, there is in us all a divine appetency, which seeks the light, which yearns for the light. We may slumber on, till it is too late; but then we must awake, and the fierce craving awakes also, and will not be denied, and there is no longer wherewith to satisfy it. So our highest capacities become our fiercest tormentors. It was an impossible prayer, which the hero breathed of old, 'Kill me, if it be only in the light.' Light, perfect light, never can be death. Life and light are synonyms in the nomenclature of the Spirit. It is the light felt and yet withheld; it is the darkness rendered visible; the helpless consciousness of spectral forms, which we may realise and yet cannot put away, haunting the gloom, that perplexes and scares and paralyses the soul.

And have we not, even in the experiences of the present, analogies, however faint, which may teach us how the most painful sight hereafter shall be the sight of Him Whom we pierced; and the wrath to come shall indeed be the wrath of the Lamb?

Is it the memory of some base ingratitude, which lies heavy on the soul? A disdainful word has been spoken, a cruel insult has been offered in a moment of irritation to the 'heart's best brother,' the friend of boyhood and youth; and they two have parted asunder, never to meet again on earth. Or was it an act of cold and defiant self-assertion, a display of heartless indifference, which was only half-meant, but which has wrung a mother's heart? And he was too proud to ask pardon, though a single word would have healed the wound, and the sore is ever festering in him. And then death comes, and in a moment an impassable barrier is reared. What would he not give then, just to unsay that cruel word, or to undo that selfish act? What sacrifice would he not then undergo, if only for a moment the impenetrable veil could be raised, and they could meet face to face as of old, so that he might pour forth a few hurried sentences of sorrow and shame, and hear from those lips the one precious word of forgiveness? But the opportunity is gone for ever. He cannot retrieve the irretrievable. And so the bright vision of the past rises up in vengeance against him, with all its sweet memories, and all its joyful hopes. The wise counsels and the affectionate greetings and the tender solicitudes, the self-denying devotion which was lavished so freely upon him—all these haunt his path, and leave him no rest. Love itself is become his tormentor. Love itself is turned into wrath.

Or again; it is not perhaps wronged affection, it is discarded innocence, which grasps the sword of the avenger, and wields it with both hands. We have read how some fallen one will revisit under cover of darkness the home of her happy childhood, and haunt the doors which are barred to her for ever, and peer stealthily through the windows that she may see the innocent faces gathered, as of old, round the fireside; or we have been taught how in the midst of splendour, after months or years of unrealised shame, some long forgotten strain of music, striking accidentally on the ear—so sweet of old, so jarring and discordant now—startles all the ghosts of the past from their graves, and no power can lay them. The conscience rebels and refuses to be drugged any more. These, it may be, are fictions of the poet and the painter; but do they not commend themselves by their absolute truthfulness? This divine paradox of retribution is manifested again and again. Again and again we are bidden to look, for the avenging Lion is there: we lift up our eyes, and 'lo, a Lamb as it had been slain.'

Yes; purity avenges itself. A man may get to think it a poor, tame, spiritless thing—one of those childish adornments, which he may cast lightly off, when he casts off the child. So he trifles with it; and in a moment of recklessness flings it away. Then comes the terrible revulsion, the sense of its priceless value, and of his own infinite loss. Then is the self-loathing and the remorse, the expulsion and the shame. He is driven forth from the garden, and the gate is barred behind him, and the flaming sword waving to and fro will not permit his return. He has tasted the tree of knowledge of good and evil, and it has cost him the tree of life. The great ideal of innocence, which he has defied, confronts him with its glory, and his eyes cannot bear the sight. All this, or nearly all this, is involved in the noble saying of the Stoic poet, who counts it the most righteous penalty which offended heaven can inflict on the hardened sinner, that he shall behold virtue, and, beholding it, pine away over the sight of his loss. All this, and far more than this, is gathered up in the prophetic vision of the Apocalypse, which is the Christian fulfilment of the Stoic's dream; 'Every eye shall see Him, even they which pierced Him.'

Far more than this; for it is possible now to put the vision aside. Experience does not teach us that in this world the intensity of the remorse is always proportionate to the gravity of the sin. A little more trifling, a little fresh indulgence; and the vision will pass away. The innocence had gone before; and now the ideal has vanished out of sight. The man has peace now, if a false security can be called peace. But what, if hereafter the veil should be suddenly plucked away? What, if the scales should fall again from his eyes? What, if the avenger should start on his feet once more, and exact the debt, swollen with the arrears of a long oblivion?

Far more than this; for the heathen poet could only contemplate virtue as a bare abstraction, beautiful indeed in itself, but hardly touching the surface of the heart. Our ideal is a Person—a Person, Who sums up in Himself all things in heaven and earth, all the magnificent teachings of science and all the inspiring lessons of history; but a Person also, Who has entered into human relations with us, Whom we have been permitted to know with our human knowledge, and to love with our human love. This it is, which must invest the sight of Him hereafter with such unspeakable awe to those who have pierced Him. For here—in this one Being—is embodied all the innocence which we have profaned, and all the truth which we have foresworn, and all the glory which we have despised. Here—in this one Man— are concentrated every blessing spurned and every opportunity lost. But above all these, crowning all and glorifying all and solemnising all, is the ideal of absolute love; the love which made its home on earth and lived a human life; the love which died for us on the Cross; the love which we might have made our own, but which we despised and flung away as a broken vessel.

This—can we doubt it—is the wrath of the Lamb. Not that He is changed, but that we are changed. He is the Lamb still. His truth, His righteousness, His purity, His love are eternal. But our perversity has transformed them into avenging angels. And so is fulfilled the saying which was written, 'With the holy thou shalt be holy...and with the froward thou shalt learn frowardness.' One sad reproachful look wrung from an Apostle bitter tears of remorseful shame. And how shall we bear that same look intensified a thousandfold and resting upon us—we who have denied Him, we who have pierced Him, we who have crucified Him afresh?

And forgive me, if I delay you a little longer, that I may make some more direct application of the lesson. I would wish more especially to speak of those privileges, which are offered to the majority of you now, and which, if neglected now, must revive and reappear in the avenging vision of the great hereafter. And here I might dwell on the magnificent opportunities of youth, on the glory of consecrating the freshness and the enthusiasm and the impressibility of early manhood to the highest of all sciences. But I abstain, simply because I know that, speaking on such a theme, I should speak to deaf ears. Any language, which I should think of using, would seem exaggerated to you young men now. A time will come, when no words will appear too extravagant for the theme; but this time is yet distant. No young man realises the glorious potentiality of youth, till youth has passed away. Therefore I will turn to other topics, which have a better chance of a hearing. And I would ask your attention chiefly to two privileges, which you enjoy here, and which you are not likely to enjoy so fully hereafter.

1. The first is the opportunity of daily prayer—more especially of daily morning prayer—in your College Chapels. Only think what a powerful instrument of self-discipline (to say nothing else) you neglect, in neglecting this! Only think what a sovereign preservative is here against sloth and all the countless vices which throng in its train! Only reflect on the glorious gain in thus dedicating publicly and solemnly the first-fruits of each day to God—what a tone of moral strength and what a well-spring of spiritual life is here! How then do you shew your appreciation of it? Will the history be this? In your first term you begin your attendance; and for a time you attend with fair regularity. But the effort is slightly irksome to you. You do not reflect that this very fact is highest testimony to its disciplinary value. So you allow yourself a little indulgence, and again

a little more; till what was the rule is now the exception, and its efficacy as a moral discipline has almost gone. And meanwhile its spiritual power too is weakened. You find that you can do very well without it; you do not seem to yourself to care very much for it. At first there was a certain sense of dissatisfaction at each fresh relaxation of the rule. But this soon wears off; and it gives you no trouble now. Have you weaned yourself from a superfluous want? Or is it not that you have stunted a divine faculty by disuse?

2. The second privilege, to which I would refer, is the opportunity of uninterrupted solitude. You have never had this opportunity in the same degree before; it is not very likely that you will continue to have it, when your residence here ceases. Your time is now almost absolutely at your own disposal. You have ample leisure to retire into yourself, to interrogate yourself, to learn of yourself. And be assured your most valuable lessons must be learnt here. I feel no temptation to depreciate the blessings of friendship. The friendships formed and cemented here are a chief glory of this place. I should do ill to undervalue the instruction derived from books. Certainly experience does not suggest the need of the warning, which Columba is said to have addressed to a pupil of old, 'My son, many out of undue love of knowledge

have made shipwreck of their souls.' It may be the temptation of a few; it is not the peril of the many. But, believe it, you can learn from yourselves lessons, more profound, more comprehensive, more abiding than any books or any friendships can teach you. Believe it—for it is truly said—each one of you is greater than he knows. This is even more true of the least gifted undergraduate in these galleries, than of the most gifted. He is far, very far, greater than he knows. Only go down deep enough into yourself, and you will find a Teacher, Whose lessons no printed page and no wise companionship can replace—for you have found there God Himself, God speaking through your individuality, God evoking your special gift, God ordering your special task.

These blessings, and such as these, I ask you to remember to-day. I did not select the text that I might enlarge on the terrors of the unseen world. I have no faith in such a mode of teaching. But I have wished to anticipate the vision of the future, that so we may more fully realise the lesson of the present; that the glory of our divine human Ideal—His holiness, His purity, His righteousness, His mercy, His love—may attract and rivet our gaze; that so beholding and worshipping and growing into the same image, we may be ready to follow Him, whithersoever He goeth, grudging no sacrifice and sparing no toil.

'And looking upon Jesus as He walked, he saith, Behold the Lamb of God!

'And the two disciples heard him speak, and they followed Jesus.'

V.

THE REVEALER OF THE HEART.

The saying of the woman, which testified, He told me all that ever I did.

S. JOHN iv. 39.

Great S. Mary's Church, 24th Sunday after Trinity, 1874.

IT is a common remark that the most momentous revolutions in history have not unfrequently sprung out of incidents altogether disproportionate to the results. This disproportion is nowhere more strongly marked than in the narrative from which the text is taken. A conversation between a Galilean carpenter and a Samaritan peasant-woman on the brink of a well—this certainly is not the occasion which we should have expected to inaugurate a revolution designed to change the religious ideas, and with them the social and political principles, of a whole civilised world. Such conversations were held many times daily over hundreds of wells in Palestine. Yet here, on this one day, at this sixth hour, near this village, Sychar, on the ledge of this particular fountain, went forth the edict, which was destined to be the one critical moment, the one absolute turning-point, in the religious history of mankind. 'The hour cometh' —not only 'cometh,' but *'now is'*—'when ye shall neither in this mountain, nor yet at Jerusalem, worship the Father.' Here is the rescission of the old order, and the charter of the new. All the old religions had been ethnic; the new must be cosmopolitan. All the old religions centred about some local sanctuary, worshipped some local power; the new religion should be wide as the overspreading sky itself, should be omnipresent and all-pervading, like the breath of the wind—the symbol of the Spirit— which bloweth where it listeth, which comes we know not whence, and goes we know not whither. Even Judaism itself was (as has been truly said) in some sense ethnic. The object of worship was indeed the One Omnipresent and Almighty, the Eternal 'I Am;' but He was worshipped still as a national God, was enshrined still in a national sanctuary. Now even these limitations should cease. The rite of initiation which inducted into the privileges of the nation should be abolished. The laws which formed the constitutional charter of the nation should be abrogated. The solid and stately edifice which was the visible centre of the nation's hopes, the local bond of the nation's unity, should be levelled with the dust. The religion of a people, of a tribe, must expand into the religion of mankind. 'Nor yet at Jerusalem'— this was the most startling paradox, the last intolerable scandal. 'Neither in this mountain'—not on yonder plateau which crowns these bare overhanging heights of Gerizim, nor on any unauthorized sanctuary like this—not on the stately hill of the Capitol or beneath the cleft-peak of Parnassus or on the steep rock-fortress of the Acropolis or in the sea-girt groves of Delos, or on the brink of the salt-marshes of Ephesus, not amidst the lofty propylaea and the colossal effigies of Memphis or of Thebes—should deity under whatever form or with whatever disguise be worshipped henceforth. So far it was a welcome truth. But this superadded clause, 'Nor yet at Jerusalem' spoilt everything. It was an outrage on the keenest hope of the Jew. And yet this unexpected, this unwelcome, this hateful edict was destined to be the saving of nations.

And on no occasion was the irony of God's munificence more signally illustrated than here. The recipients of His best treasures of revelation and of grace have rarely been those whom we should have expected beforehand. It was not here to the princes of the Hebrew hierarchy like Caiaphas, or to the leaders of Hebrew thought like Gamaliel, that the announcement was made. It was not to some Alexandrian Jew, like Philo, whose familiarity with the rich stores of Gentile learning might seem to have prepared his mind for a message of such vast import; it was not to some Platonic or Pythagorean philosopher, whose sympathies with the ancient wisdom of the farther East combining with his native Hellenic culture had enlarged his theological horizon, so that he might take in this new idea of a religion of mankind—it was not to any of these that the revelation was first made; but to a simple peasant woman, belonging to an obscure tribe hated and scorned by the Jews, who were themselves the hated and scorned of all the world—to a peasant woman, whose religious ideas shared with the rest of her people were strangely vague and confused, and whose own personal life had been stained by sins of no ambiguous hue. It seemed as if by selecting a degraded Samaritan outcast as the recipient of this gracious message to mankind, the Saviour would declare at the outset, what should be hereafter the destiny of that capacious drag-net which must sweep into its meshes of every kind. For she was the very type of the world of that day —the world which Christ came to teach and to save —whose religion was a vague compromise between the monotheism of the Jew and the pantheism of the philosopher and the idolatry of the pagan, and whose moral principles not only admitted, but even consecrated, sensuality in its most degrading forms.

But there is another very striking feature also in this narrative, which must not pass unnoticed. The intense realism which pervades every line of the Evangelist's account.

It appears first in the local scenery, which forms the setting of the history. Here by this long, dusty road, running south and north, the traveller must needs pass on his way from Jerusalem to Galilee. Here branching off westward is the narrow valley, which encloses the town of Shechem, shut in between the two parallel ridges of mountains. Here on the southern of the two heights, on this overhanging mountain of Gerizim, is the ruined temple, the sanctuary of the Samaritan race, where their 'fathers worshipped.' Here, just where the high road strikes the base of the mountain, is the little village of Askar, the Sychar of the Gospels; here hard by is a deep well, so deep even now that, notwithstanding the accumulated rubbish of ages, travellers have sounded to a depth of eighty or a hundred feet. Here stretching eastward is a sight common enough to our English eyes, but rare indeed among the bare and rocky hills of Palestine—a wide expanse of corn-land, 'unbroken' (as it is described by an eye-witness) 'by boundary or hedge'—these fields which 'are white already to harvest.'

This realism appears again in the national sentiment and traditions, with which the conversation is saturated. There is the notice of the assignment of land to Joseph, the reputed forefather of the Samaritan race. There is the allusion to the inveterate, internecine feud between the Jews and the Samaritans, which rendered any overtures from the one to the other an astonishing, if not a suspicious, incident. There is the reference to the main question of dispute between the two races—the question respecting the locality of the true sanctuary—the alternative between the mountain of Shechem and the mountain of Jerusalem. There is mention incidentally made of the vague, halting, undetermined theological position of the Samaritans—whose temple was dedicated to the 'nameless' God, and whose allegiance (at least at one time) seems to have hovered between the Jehovah of the Pentateuch and the Zeus Hellenius of Antiochus, 'Ye know not what ye worship.' There is the underlying assumption of the characteristic Samaritan conception of the Messiah, not (like the Jewish) as a magnificent king, a victorious captain, but as a teacher, a prophet, 'He will tell us all things'—a conception, to which the Samaritan was almost necessarily limited, because his

Scriptures were confined to the Pentateuch, and his Messianic ideas were all gathered from the one passage in Deuteronomy. There is an indication (in the surprise of the disciples) of the social prudery with which the rabbinical teaching had imbued the age, for a maxim of the stricter rabbis forbad any conversation in public with one of the other sex, 'They marvelled that He talked with a woman.'

It appears, lastly, in the development of the dialogue and in the progress of the event. We have a succession of rapidly shifting scenes, all equally distinct, all equally lifelike. The place, the hour, the persons; the chief Traveller throwing Himself wearily down on the well side; the disciples despatched to the neighbouring village to buy food; the approach of the woman; the conversation commenced; the ever-varying phases of emotion produced by the stranger's words; the first surprise, 'Thou, a Jew;' the surprise exchanged for remonstrance, 'Sir, the well is deep;' the prompt desire, the dawning intelligence, 'Give me this water;' the parrying of the home-thrust, 'I have no husband;' the intermingling of an eager curiosity on a great theological question with a no less eager desire to divert the conversation from an inconvenient personal turn, 'I perceive that Thou art a prophet;' the wish to evade the responsibility of a decision upon this question by indefinite postponement: 'When Messias is come, He will tell us all things;' the return of the disciples; their shocked feelings at seeing their great rabbi thus forgetting himself; the hurried departure of the woman, her pitcher left behind and her errand unfulfilled; the feminine eagerness to tell the news to her neighbours; the natural exaggeration covering the instinctive reticence, not 'He told me that I was living a life of shame,' but 'He told me all that ever I did.'

And not only is this narrative vivid and truthful in itself—truthful to natural scenery, truthful to local associations and local history, truthful to human life and character; but the allusions to place and circumstance occur in such a way as altogether to exclude the supposition of inventive design. They are not paraded before the reader; they are unexplained by themselves. Without the assistance of travellers we should often be at a loss to account for them. Of this kind is the reference to Gerizim, 'Sir, I perceive that Thou art a prophet. Our fathers worshipped in this mountain.' The context contains no indication that any mountain was near; even when mentioned, it is not mentioned by name; but the woman, suddenly looking up, sees the overhanging heights, and they suggest a ready topic, which will divert the unpleasant tenour of the conversation. Similar too is the allusion to the growing corn, 'Lift up your eyes, and look on the fields, for they are white already to harvest.' This mention is altogether unexpected, abrupt, inexplicable—inexplicable otherwise than by the actual scenery itself. The Great Teacher's eye ranges over the vast expanse of cornland, and the vision of the eye starts the lesson from the lips. The scenery does not garnish the discourse; the discourse arises out of the scenery.

What is the inference from all this? Have we here a fictitious narrative, written, as some men would tell us, by a late Christian of Gnostic tendencies, written far away from the scenes themselves, at Alexandria or in Asia Minor, written long after the supposed occurrences, somewhere about the middle of the next century, when two successive devastations under Titus and under Hadrian had harried the land, and the Jewish nation and polity were altogether a thing of the past, when in history, as in theology, old things had passed away and all things had become new.

And what analogy can be produced for such a remarkable phenomenon of literary history as this? 'The world,' it is said, 'is full of works of imagination;' 'the singular realism of many,' we are told, 'is recognised by all.' Is this a true description of the world in the early Christian centuries? Is it not the very opposite of a true description? Can even one romance of antiquity be pointed out, which approaches this in its perfect truthfulness of delineation? Even one, which offers anything like the same variety of tests, and which responds to every test applied with anything like the same fidelity? We have specimens of classical romances extant. What are they worth? 'Singular realism'—is not this the very last expression which would fitly describe them? But was it rather in Christian circles that such a wonderful product of literary genius might have been looked for? In Christian circles of the second century, which (we are reminded again and again) were notoriously careless, uncritical, inappreciative, eagerly devouring the most clumsy forgeries? In Christian circles, whose highest conception of a romance did not rise above the stiff pedantry of the Clementines, or the childish extravagance of the Protevangelium? And who was this anonymous writer, this wonderful genius, this consummate artist—if an artist, a far greater artist than Plato—whose name is nevertheless lost for ever in the greatness of the past?

Is this the probable alternative? Is it even a possible alternative? Or must we not confess that we have here the very record of a true incident, reported by an eye-witness—not, I venture to think, by Him, the chief speaker, nor by her, the chief listener, but directly by the beloved disciple himself, the youthful friend, lingering by his Master's side as not unnaturally he would linger while the others were despatched to the neighbouring village to purchase food for the common wants, suppressing the fact of his own presence in his after narrative, as characteristically he would suppress it, where the words and the incident told their own tale, and no personal attestation was needed; but listening at the time, silent, thoughtful, bewildered, amazed, and after long years recalling with all that freshness, with which old men will recall the critical moments of their boyhood and youth though the vast intervening space may be blurred and indistinct to the memory—recalling, I say, those strange sayings uttered more than half a century before on the brink of the Samaritan well—the startling announcement, 'Neither in this mountain *nor yet* at Jerusalem,' and the hardly less startling anticipation, 'The fields are white already to the harvest'—hard sayings, dark enigmas, grievous scandals, when they were at first heard; but now at length grown

Of new significance and fresh result;

now in the light of a lifelong experience, now in this far distant Gentile city of Ephesus, amidst this ever-growing congregation of Gentile Christians, gratefully acknowledged as the manifesto of a new revelation and the charter of a new Church. A true son of Thunder, whose work in life is typified, not by the ceaseless din as of some busy machinery, but by the deafening clap and the vivid flash which, sudden and intermittent, startles the silence of a summer sky.

The context has brought us to the outskirts of Christian evidences. The text itself penetrates to their very core: 'He told me all that ever I did:' 'He tore away the veil of disguise, which I had so carefully wrapped about me. He exposed my secret life; He probed my inmost conscience; He held up a mirror to me, and for the first time I saw myself.' This unique power of piercing, wounding, exposing, convicting, convincing the conscience is, and ever must be, the most potent testimony to the revelation in Christ.

Christian evidences! How few have the time, have the opportunities, have the capacities, have the training, necessary for a right judgment on the subjects submitted to them! And yet to the many the truth of Christianity is a question not less momentous than to those few. Here then is their evidence. It presupposes no long intellectual discipline; it demands no unusual mental powers; it draws on no rich accumulation of knowledge. It addresses itself to the poor, to the simple, to the ignorant. It appealed to this unlettered Samaritan peasant, with the same directness of aim, as to a Hillel or a Gamaliel; to this shamed and sullied profligate with the same distinctness of articulation as to the most scrupulous, most respectable, most orthodox of Pharisees. 'He spoke to my conscience; He shewed me my sin; He shewed me myself. He told me all things that ever I did.'

And this is not only the most simple and comprehensive, it is also the most forcible and the most convincing of all kinds of evidence. Let any one test the truth of this by his own past experience. Let him only recall some one rare moment in the past; when the conviction of sin, the revelation of self, was flashed in upon his soul: when suddenly the dishonesty, the hypocrisy, the malice, the avarice, the impurity, the meanness, the sin (whatever it may have been), which he had so long indulged with so much self-complacency, rose up before him with a terrible distinctness of outline, confronting him, as it were, with a second self. Long lapse of time, worldly cares, dissipating interests, indifference, recklessness, may now have confused the memory. But then he could not deceive himself. It was no phantom of a diseased imagination. It was an intensely real, intensely true, experience; it was direct, it was personal, it was absolute. He had seen the exceeding sinfulness of sin; he had been confronted with the great mystery of iniquity. And he could no more doubt the reality of the power, which had revealed it to him, than he could doubt the force of gravitation itself. 'He told me all things that ever I did. Is not this, yes, is not this the Christ?'

We have been reading lately some speculations on the utility of religion. The honest utterance of a singularly honest mind is always a substantial gain. It goes to increase the store of trustworthy data, on which the judgments of mankind must be built. And in this case the value is enhanced, because the voice speaks to us (as it were) from beyond the grave. But was adequacy, or any approach to adequacy, in the treatment, to be anticipated here? The utility of religion depends on the power of religion. And the power of religion can only be estimated by inward experience. It must ever be a matter of personal testimony. It cannot be weighed and tabulated.

Intrinsically faulty then, because entirely speculative, must be the estimate of one, who (as he himself frankly confesses) never had a faith to lose, who even in these his posthumous utterances is still feeling after a religion, not denying it as a possibility, but relegating it to the cloudland of peradventure, and allowing it, nay even encouraging it, as a salutary play of the imagination.

Hence, in the Essay to which I have referred, I

find something said, and not absolutely untruly, about the insufficiency of the fear of future punishment regarded as a moral police. I find a little said, though altogether inadequately, about the influence of a noble ideal in attracting men to virtue. But I find nothing at all on this one point—the power of religion in penetrating, revealing, shaming, purifying, exalting the inner life through the conviction of sin, and the craving after righteousness. And yet every Christian knows that this is after all the most potent, because the most subtle, influence which acts upon his moral being—penetrating into recesses where all others must fail, touching springs of action which none other can reach. He is not ungrateful for external supports. He sees well enough, how very much he owes to the force of law, or of public opinion, as the scaffolding of his moral nature. But he cannot deceive himself. He knows that whole regions of moral life lie far beyond the reach of any such forces. He knows how many an evil thought he puts away, how many an alluring temptation he resists, how many a painful struggle he undergoes, how many a distasteful task he undertakes—not at all because public opinion expects it of him (public opinion knows nothing of all this); not at all because the terror of a future judgment haunts him (the thought is far away from his mind); but because he is conscious of a Presence, pleading with him, admonishing him, alluring him, entreating him, startling him by the heinousness of his sin, reflected in the mirror of a perfect righteousness. He cannot deceive himself. He knows, as certainly as he knows anything, how very far worse he would have been if this voice had been silent, if this Presence had been withdrawn. He sees that he is only one unit among myriads. He reflects that this motive has been far more potent with thousands upon thousands of men than (to his shame) it has been with himself. And reflecting on all this, he feels that he cannot place any bounds to the utility of religion regarded as a moral force. For the mainspring of all this power is the revelation of self through the revelation of God in Christ. 'He gave me the answer to that twofold question, the question of all questions, 'Whence?' and 'Where?' He shewed me all the mercy, for He told me all the sin. He convinced me of my greatness, for He convicted me of my meanness. He set before me the image of perfect holiness, embodied in a Man like myself. Then He shewed me my own sinful heart, my own sullied life. It was a contrast of light and darkness. I could not choose but hate the darkness and love the light. And so in my poor, feeble, halting way I am feeling for the light, I am straining after the light. He told me all that ever I did. Is not this the Christ?'

And with this conviction kindling within him, he hurries out into the world. He becomes perforce a missionary and an apologist—a missionary, though not perhaps across the seas or amidst deserts; an apologist, though not in the pulpit or with his pen— but he pleads with the resistless eloquence of a direct personal knowledge; he argues with the overpowering logic of a renewed and purified life. His secret is bursting within him, and he must impart it to others. He arrests, he appeals, he importunes. 'Come, see a man, which told me all things that ever I did. Come, see and hear and judge for yourselves. Is not this the Christ?'

VI.

THE MEANNESS AND THE GREATNESS OF MAN.

What is man, that Thou art mindful of him: and the son of man, that Thou visitest him?

PSALM viii. 4.

Great S. Mary's Church, 2nd Sunday after Easter, 1876.

WHO is here the speaker? Are we reading the experiences of the stripling still watching over his father's flocks by night in the upland pastures of Bethlehem? Or of the lonely fugitive contemplating the starry skies from the broad plains of Philistia? Or of the powerful sovereign gazing upward to the overhanging vault from the palace roofs of Zion? Whether David the shepherd lad, or David the outlaw, or David the king, it matters not. The central idea of this magnificent psalm is plainly expressed, and makes no demands on historical criticism for its elucidation. Surveying the outspread canopy of heaven, the Psalmist is overwhelmed with awe at the scene. Its vast expanse, its fathomless blue, its starry glories, its beauty, its purity, its repose, all appal him with the sense of their grandeur; and crushed with the contrast between the greatness of universal creation and the littleness of the individual man, he exclaims bewildered and amazed, 'When I consider Thy heavens, the work of Thy fingers, the moon and the stars, which Thou hast ordained; what is man that Thou art mindful of him, and the son of man that Thou visitest him? Mystery of mysteries, that one so mean—an atom in this limitless expanse, a mote in this faultless glory, a flutter in this infinite calm—should be singled out for Thy special favour, and endowed with authority as Thy vicegerent upon earth.' Could any paradox be imagined greater than this—this contrast, between the insignificance of man's self and the pre-eminence of man's destiny?

We pass from the early dawn to the late afternoon of human history. The lapse of eight-and-twenty centuries is a large space in the life of mankind. It is a vast and profound chasm, which separates the simple inspiration of the shepherd-king from the many-sided culture of the poet, critic, philosopher, novelist, scientific investigator, the typical representative of modern thought and intellect in its latest phases. Yet to Goethe, holding solitary communion with nature in its higher forms, and contemplating earth and sky from the summit of the Brocken, the Psalmist's thought still recurs with resistless importunity and finds its natural expression still in the Psalmist's words, 'Lord, what is man, that Thou art mindful of him?' No interval of time nor transference of scene, no contrast of persons or of circumstances has tarnished its freshness, or robbed it of its power.

Has robbed it of its power? Nay, must we not rather confess, in very truth, that as the world has grown older, the chasm between the greatness and the meanness of man has widened, and the paradox has increased from age to age? Was this disproportion so startling as to perplex and overawe the mind of the simple Hebrew in the remote past? What must it not be to us, who measure it by the accumulated experience of all the ages? This is the very essence of a true inspiration, that it should speak with fuller tones and a more articulate utterance to after-ages, than to the generations to which it was immediately addressed. So it is here. Every acquisition of modern science has emphasized the contrast in a manner which the Psalmist himself could not have foreseen. Each new discovery has depressed the relative importance of man in the material universe. Each fresh investigation has obliterated some external distinction of origin or of structure or of growth, which was thought to isolate him from the rest of creation. Again and again, as science has announced some fresh revelation, the mysterious paradox has been brought home to our minds with redoubled force, 'Lord, what, *what* is man, that Thou art mindful of him?'

1. Astronomy first issued her impressive comment on the text, and the Christian teachers have not been slow to adopt her forcible illustrations of its truth. The starry heavens were a panorama of unspeakable beauty and awe to the shepherd-king nearly·three thousand years ago. What must they not be to us now? We know now—any well-instructed child knows now—that those bright specks, which appeared to his eye as jewels studding the midnight sky, are glorious suns, the centres, it may be, round which are revolving worlds as huge and as magnificent as our own. We know now that, where he discerned only one such speck, there are thousands of these separate suns. We know now that those irregular patches of hazy light so shapeless and so unmeaning, which appear only to dim the purity of the liquid sky, are aggregates of such stars or

suns, countless in multitude. We know now the smallest of the visible stars to be so remote that even with the extraordinary speed of light a ray flashed from one of these, when David was king, cannot even yet have reached our eyes. These truths are now the simplest educational lessons; and yet they never pall upon the imagination. As the long rows of figures, which describe the distances, are arrayed before us, and we vainly strive to grasp some conception of the facts which they represent, the eye swims and the mind falters. Racked with the vastness of these reasonings, we resign the hopeless task in despair; and the saying of the Psalmist presses upon us with crushing force, 'Lord, what is man, amidst these countless worlds? What is man, nay, what is all humanity, but an atom in this limitless universe, a drop in this ocean of infinite space?'

2. And, before we have recovered from our amazement and collected our stupefied senses, Geology takes up the lesson which Astronomy has laid down, enforcing it with other and not less striking illustrations. Geology teaches us our insignificance in time, as Astronomy had taught us our insignificance in space. Geology tells us how this earth, of which we boast ourselves the lords paramount, as if by the indefeasible title of sole and undisputed possession,

existed for countless ages before the creation of our race. She relates how through millions of years continents were made and unmade, mountains piled up and seas poured out, climates changed from frigid to torrid and from torrid to frigid, new creations of vegetable and animal life peopled the earth and lived out their time and died off in endless succession; till once more the mind, wearied with the effort to grasp the vastness of the idea, resigns its functions; and this new announcement again wrings from us the despairing cry, 'What is man? What is man, even on this earth of his own, but a fleeting apparition, a thing of yesterday, one term in an endless series, one ripple on the stream of the ages, one moment in infinite time?'

3. But again: before we have had time to realise this fresh comment on the text, the teaching of the Psalmist is enforced anew from quite another quarter. As the telescope had revealed to us vast and multitudinous worlds stretching out into boundless space, so the microscope discovers to us miniature worlds equally strange and unsuspected, crowding under our very eyes, countless in number and each thronged with a dense population of its own. A single drop of water appears peopled with thousands of minute living creatures, which multiply indefinitely with the increased power of our lenses. A single nodule of

rock is seen to be composed of millions of fossil organisms, each one endowed with a vitality of its own. Everywhere is life, teeming, fermenting, inexhaustible life. And so once more our imagination sinks under the burden of the thought, and once more we echo the cry of humiliation, 'Lord, what is man? What is man, but a single throb in this endless pulsation of nature, a solitary bubble on this effervescence of infinite, omnipresent life?'

4. Nor is this all. Hitherto at least the main fortress of our pride is unassailed. We can still maintain the isolation, the uniqueness, of man in the physical creation. But even this fondly-cherished idea falls before the next assault of science. The anatomist dissects and the chemist analyses the human body. This complex mechanism, this marvellous tenement of the spirit, is resolved into its component elements. Now at least it would seem as though the secret must be revealed. Now at length we shall discover whence comes, and wherein resides, and what *is*, the distinctive glory of man. Now at length we shall be able to hold up to the eye, and submit to the touch, the evidence of his special pre-eminence. But here too we are doomed to disappointment. Our expected triumph becomes a signal defeat. The elements of the human body are analysed and sorted and weighed and tabulated.

Man is found to be compounded of just such substances as the brute or the tree or the stone. There is absolutely nothing besides. Reason, memory, imagination, foresight, spirit, conscience, personality —they are not here. Had we any right to expect it otherwise? This is no newly-discovered truth. It is as ancient as the first promptings of inspiration. It was declared, as in a parable, in that Divine saying of old, 'Dust thou art, and unto dust shalt thou return.' But it comes home to us with redoubled force, when the dissecting room and the laboratory have done their work; and nothing has been laid bare by the scalpel, and nothing has been detected by the retort, which can explain the mystery of man's being—no unique atom which is the abode of the spirit, no nucleus which contains the living, thinking man, no indiscerptible unit, of which philosophers have dreamed, as the palpable germ of his immortality. 'What is your life? It is even a vapour that appeareth for a little time, and then vanisheth away;' and the mocking echo of materialism gives back the Apostle's saying, 'even a vapour, that vanisheth away.' 'What is man? An aggregate of chemical elements nicely combined, a compound of evanescent gases which escape and are dissipated, and all is gone.'

5. Once more. If there is nothing in the

component elements of the human frame which accounts for the pre-eminence of man, we may at all events look for an explanation in some peculiarities of structure. We shall at least find some differentiating characteristic here: we shall detect a certain uniqueness of type, which explains all. At length we shall have laid our finger on the elusive secret. Comparative anatomy and comparative physiology will come to our aid, where other sciences have failed us. This is our last hope; but here too we are frustrated. Each fresh advance of science seems to shew more plainly that we must look elsewhere than to his physical structure and growth for an explanation of the man, as the ruling, thinking, progressive, immortal being. The naturalist will tell us that the same essential type of structure prevails throughout; that different parts are more or less fully developed in different creatures, but that the ground idea in all is identical. He will tell us that the individual human being has in the several stages of his growth passed through forms analogous to the several types of the lower animals, before his structure was completed. He will tell us that all attempts at classification with a view to separating man off by a broad line from the lower creation fail signally. A slightly different convolution of the brain, a slightly different conformation of the skull, a firmer grasp of

the hand, a steadier gait of the foot— trifles these—
yet these, and such as these, are all that he can find
to distinguish the man from the brute. And perhaps
he will boldly advance a theory that the man is after
all only the brute developed through a long series of
ages. Of the truth or the falsehood of such a theory
I say nothing here. But if it should prove most true,
would it not justify and enforce by a new and unsuspected illustration the Psalmist's awe, while contemplating the contrast between the nature and the
destiny of man? 'Man being in honour abideth
not: he is like the beasts that perish.' And again
the voice of materialism throws back his pious
ejaculation with its mocking echo, 'like the beasts
that perish.' 'What is man? Half-akin, nay more
than half-akin, to the brute. And the son of man?
A superior mammal, a developed mollusc, a creature
among creatures, a finer sample of a vulgar type.'

Thus again and again we are brought back to the
same point. Again and again, as we contemplate
some new revelation of science, our amazement grows.
At each step we are more and more bewildered with
this strange paradox of humanity, this contrast between the two elements in our nature—that which we
have in common with the lower creation, and that
which is our special endowment as men—the dust
which is taken from the earth, and the spirit which is

breathed into us by God. At each step we exclaim with increased intensity of wonder, 'What is man, that Thou art mindful of him: and the son of man, that Thou visitest him?'

For we cannot stop short at the first clause of the Psalmist's words, and refuse to entertain the sequel. The materialist will be content to say, 'What is man? An insignificant atom in time and space. And the son of man? An organism like other organisms.' But the believer is constrained to add, 'Lord, that Thou art mindful of him! Lord, that Thou visitest him!' It is just this addition which transmutes the sneer of a cynical contempt, or the wail of a prostrate despair, into the psalm of devout and reverential awe.

And the believer may boldly claim science herself as his teacher. To hear some men talk, one would suppose that in the height of scientific discovery the mystery of man's being had been found no mystery at all. A moment's thought will dispel the illusion. The profound secret remains as dark and impenetrable as ever. Much has been done to explain the conditions of life; but nothing, absolutely nothing, to explain life itself. Nay, every step in advance has only increased the paradox and widened the gulf, so that the mystery is more complete than before.

It has widened the gulf; for while it has shewn that man, as a material structure, is only an infinitely small fraction of a vast universe like himself, differing almost inappreciably from other fractions, it has accumulated evidence at every step, that, as a thinking, hoping, aspiring, progressive being, he is quite unique in God's creation. Each successive triumph of science makes the distance between the man and the brute wider. Each new acquisition is a fresh proof of capacity and a fresh ground for hope. If experience discovers the littleness of man to be more little, yet at the same time it shews his greatness to be more great. The Psalmist's expression of wonder and awe and thanksgiving was wrung from him chiefly by the thought, that his Almighty Creator had given to man —to man, this frail, fleeting, impotent being—the dominion over the beasts of the field and the fowls of the air and the fishes of the sea, over creatures stronger in limb and more fleet of foot and keener-sighted and better-armed and longer-lived than himself. But what is all this compared with the triumphs which we have witnessed—the sovereignty of man asserted over the elemental powers of nature? We have lived to see how he can order the lightning; commanding it, and it flashes his message from continent to continent; forbidding it, and it glances harmlessly away. We have seen him weigh the sun, and measure the heavens, and analyse the stars. We have witnessed how he has made the vapour his slave, bidding it carry him to and fro and furnish his every need. And we feel that these achievements are only an earnest of greater triumphs yet in store for humanity. While the bee constructs its cells with just the same mathematical precision, and the ant piles up its winter stores with just the same prudent foresight —neither more nor less—as they did thousands of years ago; while the horse and the dog seem to contract almost human sensibilities by association with man, and then, when they are turned wild, lose them again, as if they had been only a reflection of a human master's presence; while all the lower creation is stationary, mankind is rapidly advancing higher and higher. And still the marvel increases, 'Lord, what is man, that Thou art mindful of him, and the son of man, that Thou visitest him?—visitest him in this faculty of experience whereby he records and treasures up the accumulated wisdom of the past, visitest him in this divination of foresight wherewith he projects himself into the triumphs and the hopes of the future, visitest him in his scientific achievements, in his social progress, in his ever-extended dominion over the material universe?' Such thoughts as these may well occupy our minds. We cannot afford to overlook them. They are directly suggested by the Psalmist's hymn of praise. They must ever supply a stanza—though not the loftiest—in our song of thanksgiving to the Almighty Creator.

For after all, these magnificent victories, this dominion over the beasts of the field, this subjugation of the powers of nature, are only the earnest, the prelude, the foreshadowing, of greater things yet to come. This is plainly the Psalmist's idea. A larger, fuller, more triumphant thought is struggling for utterance, than finds direct expression in words; 'Thou hast crowned him with glory and honour; Thou hast put all things under his feet.' Hence Apostles and Evangelists saw the true fulfilment of the Psalmist's prophetic saying in the ultimate and supreme destiny of mankind, as realised in the Person and work of the one Representative Man. Nothing short of this could satisfy the hopes, which the jubilant strain inspires. Here at length was the exaltation, the glory, the absolute sovereignty, the final apotheosis of man.

And, emphasized by this comment, the song of the Psalmist falls on the ears of Christians now, with a fuller cadence, swelled with the experience of nearly thirty centuries and prolonged into the hopes of eternity, 'Lord, that Thou art mindful of him; Lord, that Thou visitest him!'

'That Thou art mindful of him.' That Thou hast condescended to hold communion with This Thy frail and sinful creature; that through long ages Thou didst school him to an ever fuller knowledge of Thee; that even in the darkest times and among the most degraded peoples Thou didst not leave Thyself without a witness, speaking through the promptings of the conscience, speaking through the courses of the seasons, speaking through the hopes and the fears of the present; that Thou didst single out one man, one family, one nation, to be the depositary of Thy special revelation; that Thou didst guard and preserve this nation through unparalleled vicissitudes, so that exiled, enslaved, crushed, trampled under foot, it revived again and again; that Thou didst from time to time commission Thy special messengers—lawgiver, psalmist, prophet, priest—to renew the flame of truth on the altar of Thy chosen race; and that thus Thy revelation burst out ever and again with a clearer, brighter light, and Thy Divine economy broadened down from precedent to precedent, till at length the religion of a nation should become the religion of the world.

'That Thou hast visited him.' That Thou didst effect this change by a signal manifestation of Thyself; that in the fulness of time, when Egyptians and Assyrians and Persians, when Greeks and Romans had prepared the way, Thou didst of Thine infinite mercy send Thine only Son upon earth; that He was born as a man, lived as a man, suffered and died as a man; and that thus by this one act of marvellous condescension, humanity was redeemed, was exalted, was sanctified.

'That Thou hast visited him.' Not only that this Thy blessed Son lived and died as a man; but that as a man He rose from the grave, and thus as a man won for men the victory over sin and death; that, as a man, He ascended into the heaven of heavens, the firstfruits of the final triumph of mankind, the earnest of that glorious consummation of all human history, when His brother-men united in Him shall wear His crown, and reign with Him as kings for ever and ever. Lord, what is man—this speck in boundless space, this moment in infinite time, this atom of atoms, this frail, fleeting, helpless creature, this insignificance, this nothing—that Thou hast ordained him to such unspeakable glory?

'What is man?' Nay, what is *this* man? What am I, that Thou visitest *me*? We cannot escape the moral of the Psalmist's appeal under the shelter of a vague generality. To you and to you—to each individually—the shaft strikes home. What am I—I with these vile passions, I with this hateful selfishness, I with this hopeless, intolerable meanness, of which I am conscious every hour, that Thou art mindful of me, that Thou visitest me? A pessimist you must be in one sense, if you examine yourself candidly. A pessimist the spirit of the time will tend to make you in another direction. It is the special temptation of our age, that its most prominent scientific interests almost of necessity lead the mind to dwell too exclusively on the lower affinities of our nature—on our animal emotions, on our perishable bodies, on our resemblance to the brute creation, on our sensitiveness, even our moral sensitiveness, to the manifold changes of circumstance, as food and climate and scenery. The danger is imminent. The thoughts, which absorb you, will also mould you. If you get to regard yourself as mean, you will at length become mean. Lift up your eyes then from earth to heaven. Rise from the consideration of your littleness to the contemplation of your greatness. Here, in that noblest of all optimisms, which science suggests and consciousness demands and revelation affirms—the belief in the unique personality, the boundless capacity, the triumphant progress, the eternal destiny of man: the belief in the godlike, nay, in the God.within you—is the saving of your soul.

The God within you. The Stoic of old would remind his disciples that they carried about a god enshrined in their hearts. Even as a vague surmise, a highly-wrought metaphor, the expression of an unsatisfied spiritual yearning, this teaching was very far from inoperative. What may it not be to you to whom it is an assured truth, to you who have been re-stamped in Christ with the image of God, to you who have been re-consecrated as the temples of the Spirit?

The God within you. Carry this thought back to your rooms, you young men, and contemplate it with all reverence on your knees. Whatever temptations may assault you, it has power to overcome them all. If every other diversion and every other remedy should fail, this will never fail. Though the craven fear of detection should not restrain you, and the noble egotism of self-respect should not uphold you, and the apprehension of consequences now or hereafter should not deter you, the awe, the majesty, the glory of this Presence realised must scare away the demons of sin from your heart. 'Lord, what are we, what am I, that Thou visitest me, that Thou makest Thine abode with me, that Thou hast enshrined Thyself in me? What are we, and what art Thou, O Lord? We are of yesterday; Thou art from eternity. We are here; Thou art everywhere. Our meanness and our greatness, our failures and our triumphs, what seems our weakness and what seems our worth—these are both alike, for these are both as nothing, in the face of Thine infinite perfection.

Grant, Lord, that we may feel and know this. Teach us, Lord, to forget ourselves in Thee, that so losing ourselves we may truly find ourselves. This is the first and last thought in the Psalmist's hymn of praise; this must be the first and the last also in the Christian's song of thanksgiving—not our meanness, not our greatness, not ourselves, not humanity, not man; but Thou and Thou only, the Alpha and the Omega, the beginning and the end; Jehovah our Lord, how excellent is Thy name in all the earth!'

VII.

OFFENCES.

It must needs be that offences come; but woe to that man by whom the offence cometh!

S. MATTHEW xviii. 7.

Great S. Mary's Church, 19th Sunday after Trinity, 1876.

THIS passage belongs at once to the most transparent and the most abstruse of our Lord's sayings. On the one hand, it is a simple statement of fact and a plain lesson of duty. Here it is so clear, that a little child may read and understand. On the other, it involves a startling antithesis, which has been the great enigma of all moral and religious philosophy from the beginning of time. There it is so inscrutable, that the most profound intellects have vainly sought to fathom its depths. Offences are a necessity, and yet offences must not be. Scandals are permitted, and yet they are forbidden. God's government presupposes evil; for otherwise no moral probation were possible. And yet God's righteousness punishes evil, for otherwise God would no longer be God. There is a law of averages, which teaches that in a given state of society a certain number of crimes will be committed in a fixed time; and yet there is a law of Divine retribution, which condemns each individual offender who contributes his quota to this aggregate. God hates sin, and yet God allows sin. This is the contradiction involved in the text. The enigma is stated, but it is not explained. Christianity did not create the difficulty, and Christianity does not offer to solve it.

But I have no desire to enter into these dark problems of religious philosophy. Standing now on the threshold of a new Academical year, and meeting together as we have met to-day in this church, many of us for the first time, we can ill afford to devote this Sunday of all Sundays to fruitless speculation. To one, who has been resident in this place and watched the ceaseless ebb and flow of University life now for nearly thirty years; who has witnessed generation after generation of young men come and go in rapid sequence; who, amidst many moral victories achieved here in each successive generation, has seen not a few glorious hopes disappointed, not a few brilliant promises unfulfilled, not a few noble characters (or such as might have been noble) debased, and who therefore feels with an intensity which younger men cannot be expected to share, that this first entrance on Academic life, like all great opportunities, is in the truest sense to each man, according as he may use it, either a savour of life unto life or a savour of death unto death; to one, I say, upon whom the occasion forces such thoughts as these, the text cannot but suggest a simpler treatment. It must needs be that the evil example of older students—the idleness, the dissipation, the moral recklessness, the religious indifference—shall lead many astray; but woe alike to those who are led astray, and to those who lead them astray. It must needs be that many a father's reasonable hope will be belied, and many a mother's earnest prayer will be frustrated, that the dearest sanctities of many a home will be spurned; but woe unto that son nevertheless by whom they are spurned. It must needs be that many a bright intellect will be darkened by indolence or by dissipation; but woe unto him in whom it is darkened. It must needs be that many a religious faith will be lost by apathy and neglect; but woe unto him by whom it is lost. It must needs be that God's choicest gift of youth, with its bright hopes and its magnificent possibilities, will be sullied and trampled under foot as a vile thing, when it should have been consecrated to its Giver in all the freshness of its glory; but woe unto him who tramples it under foot. It must needs be that God's image, stamped on many a soul, will be ruthlessly effaced; but woe nevertheless, thrice woe, to him by whom it is effaced.

And so, with this fatal necessity and this unequivocal warning—thus illustrated by each successive year of Academic history—in his mind, the preacher will not aspire on this day to argue as a wise man with wise men. His ambition will be rather to speak as a little child to little children; content, and more than content, if some one word thrown out at a venture shall have served to warn, to deter, to sustain, to encourage, one single hearer, and thus have helped him forward to the attainment of those priceless blessings, moral, intellectual, spiritual, which lie within the reach of such as use the opportunities of their residence here aright.

As a little child to little children. Forgive me the comparison. I can frame no better prayer for you and for myself, than that we should approach this subject in this spirit. Is there something jarring and dissonant in this language at a season which is regarded by so many as the initiation into the freedom and the privileges of manhood? Nay; if there is a seeming contradiction in terms, there is entire harmony in thought. Believe it; the poet's saying is true in more senses than one that 'the child is father to the man.' There can be no true manliness, where the childlike nature is absent. The little child is the hero of Christ's panegyric in the context. The little child is the type of the citizen of God's kingdom. Its simplicity, its innocence, its frankness, its truthfulness, are the badges of civic privilege in this heavenly polity.

And, as the child is the subject of the encomium in the context, so is it also the occasion of the warning in the text. It is the stumbling-block placed in the way of Christ's little ones, that calls down the denunciation of woe. We may resent the imputation of a childish nature. We may throw off its noble characteristics; but its feebler qualities will cling to us still. All—even the strongest—have some element of weakness in their character, which renders them dependent on others. Imitation is the law of the child's nature. The most powerful instrument in moulding its character is example. It cannot understand abstract principles; but it is keenly sensible to personal influence. Its ideal is to be like its father or its mother; its constant effort is to copy an elder brother or an elder sister. In this respect the childlike never will be outgrown either in the Church or in mankind at large. The force of example will always be more potent than the most earnest appeals of the preacher and the most convincing logic of the apologist. Personal influence is as contagious as the atmosphere which envelopes us. We drink it in at every breath. We are bathed in it day and night. Precept and exhortation are momentary and fitful; but this is at all times and in all places. We can none of us escape from it. Hence the category of Christ's little ones is as wide as the Church is wide, as mankind is wide. We are all exposed to the force of some stronger nature than our own—stronger in intellect, or stronger in moral character and definiteness of purpose, or stronger (it may be) in mere passion of temperament—attracting us to the good, or impelling us to the evil. Thus in all ages doing has been more eloquent than preaching. The blood of the martyrs, not the ink of the apologists, was declared to be the seed of the Church.

Hence the severity of the language in the woe denounced against those who offend Christ's little ones. It is better for all such that they should be sunk countless fathoms deep in the sea; better that they should be put out of sight for ever; better for themselves and for others that they should be annihilated, if that were possible, than that they should any longer vex the earth with their presence.

And with the accumulated experience of eighteen centuries, who will venture to say that this warning was unneeded? The annals of the Church are blackened with crimes, committed not only by Christians but committed in the sacred name of Christ Himself. The scandals of Christendom have been far more deadly to the souls of men than the fiercest onslaughts of persecution. The one may have slain its thousands, but the other has slain its tens of thousands. We Englishmen have listened of late with a shudder of abhorrence to the reports of wholesale barbarities committed by men of an alien race and an alien religion. These butcheries, and worse than butcheries, have called forth a cry of righteous indignation throughout the country. It was an intolerable thought that Christian England should be charged with complicity, however remote, in such inhuman crimes.

But is there not a danger lest this sentiment, however healthy in itself, should encourage in us Christians a self-complacency, to which the history of the past challenges our right? Are the pages even of our ecclesiastical annals so clean, that we can arrogate to ourselves a monopoly of humane sentiments and impulses? Have we forgotten the sarcasm of the Apostate Emperor, when he claims the gratitude of the 'Galileans' for restoring peace to many provinces, which under his predecessors had been devastated by their own internal feuds, whole villages having been razed to the ground in these deadly quarrels of the Christians? Have we overlooked the cynical close of a famous chapter in the 'Decline and Fall,' where it is reckoned that 'the number of Protestants who were executed' for their religion in the sixteenth century 'in a single province and a single reign far exceeded that of the primitive martyrs in the space of three centuries and of the Roman Empire?' There may be much exaggeration in both these indictments; but the main fact is beyond contradiction. *Pudet haec opprobria nobis.* Shame on us Christians, that these things could be said, and could not be refuted. Cast your eye down the columns of Christian history, and see how century after century they are reddened with the stains of blood. The Church had scarcely been enfranchised, when the civilized world was scandalized by the riots which accompanied the election of the chief bishop of Christendom. Churches were turned into fortresses and strewn with corpses; the streets of Rome streamed with the blood of the rival partizans; while the heathen looked on with impartial scorn. Advance from the fourth century to the fifth, from Rome to Alexandria; and mark the deadly tumults which have left an indelible stain on the Church, and in which the murder of Hypatia was only an isolated, though a prominent, incident. Follow the stream of history through the succeeding centuries; and see how the powerful sovereigns, the champions of Christendom, carried the Gospel of peace everywhere at the point of the sword. Of Charles the Great it is recorded, as a merit, that he offered to his heathen foes the alternative of Christianity or extinction. And this programme was rigorously carried out. Whole tribes were ruthlessly slaughtered by this 'Mohammedan Apostle of the Gospel.' Go forward still through the centuries, and see what scenes rise up before your eyes. I say nothing of those religious wars waged against the Saracen in the East, because with all their crimes they were redeemed in part by a noble spirit of chivalry and self-devotion. But witness that so-called Crusade against the Albigenses in the early years of the thirteenth century. What would be the cry of horror throughout Europe if in to-morrow's telegrams we should read this announcement, 'A general massacre was permitted; men, women and children were cut to pieces, till there remained nothing to kill except the garrison and others reserved for a more cruel fate. Four hundred were burned in one great pile, which made a wonderful blaze and caused universal rejoicing in the camp?' And yet this is only one incident in that terrible war of extermination against the heretics, which counted its victims by tens of thousands, which made no distinction of age or sex, which shrunk from no atrocities, till the spiritual chief of Christendom himself stood aghast at the excesses of the champions whom he had hounded on, but whom he was powerless to control. And these horrors were perpetrated in the name of Him, Who refused to call down fire on that churlish Samaritan village. This diabolical energy of persecution raged under the shadow of the Cross, the very symbol of patient suffering and self-denying love. And, if it were not sickening to wade through lakes of Christian blood, I would ask you to pass with me from the thirteenth century to the sixteenth, and witness the atrocities of that terrible period— the wholesale executions in the Netherlands, whether fifty thousand or a hundred thousand, it matters not; the ceaseless flames of the Inquisition in Spain; the one terrible night of butchery in Paris, a combination of treachery and ferocity, such as the world has rarely witnessed: gigantic horrors these, before whose glare the fires of Smithfield pale into nothing, notwithstanding that they have lighted in the heart and the intelligence of England a candle which shall never be put out. Why have I dwelt so long on these painful incidents? Not, assuredly, because the Gospel is chargeable with any portion of these crimes.

Those who have studied Church history with care will see for themselves, that the barbarities of half-savage nations would have been still more barbarous, and the passions of lawless men still more passionate, if its influence had been withdrawn. Not, certainly, because these facts, truly weighed, are any argument in the hands of unbelievers. I know no stronger evidence of the inherent power and vitality of Christianity, than that it should have triumphed over these scandals of Christendom. But it is well that at a time like the present these painful memories should step in, and check our self-complacency. The atrocities of Islam have copied only too faithfully the atrocities of Christendom. And they can at least plead consistency. We did these things in defiance of our creed; while they have done them in obedience to their creed.

Surely never was there a time, when Christendom was more directly called to humble herself in the dust than when this painful likeness—this hideous caricature, if you will—of her own misdeeds is flaunted before her eyes.

And to each of us individually his share of the humiliation must fall. We would fain hope that a repetition of scandals on this vast scale among Christian nations is henceforward impossible. But still the terrible catalogue of offences is lengthening day by day. Still Christ's little ones are falling by thousands on all sides. Still the woe is gathering strength and volume for discharge. For, though the form of the scandal may change, the spirit which creates it remains; the partisanship, the falsehood, the insincerity, the bigotry, the cruelty, the pride, the self-seeking, the self-indulgence, thwarting and neutralising by its example the faith which it professes. There is the Christian apologist, who wields the weapons of disingenuousness and fraud in defence of the truth; there is the Christian preacher, whose words are words of lofty self-denial and devotion, and whose life is worldliest of the worldly; there is the Christian philanthropist, whose sympathy for the suffering and oppressed classes is unbounded, and whose bearing is morose, selfish, intolerable, in his own household; there is the Christian colonist, whose rapacity or whose lawlessness or whose tyranny makes the Sacred Name, which he bears, a byword and an abomination to the heathen among whom he dwells. These and a thousand other forms of scandal are working their deadly work; while with ever-growing importunity the cry of Christ's little ones fallen and engulfed rises up to the Eternal Throne, 'Lord, how long?'

And surely nowhere else should the warning in the text find a prompter hearing than in this place.

It is declared to be the natural constitution of the Church of Christ, that when one member suffers, all the members shall suffer with it. A University, still more a College is, as it were, a Church within a Church. The connexion of the members is closer. The contagion of sympathy, whether for good or for evil, is more immediate. The force of personal example is more directly felt. The freedom and the closeness of intercourse combines with the age of the great majority of its members to render it keenly susceptible of such influences.

And let no man think that he can escape responsibility in this matter. There is some element of strength in all, even the very weakest. It may be superior intellectual power or higher mental culture; it may be a wider acquaintance with the world; it may be more enlarged religious views; it may be a capacity of winning affection or of commanding popularity; it may be superior age or longer residence in this place. In some way or other each man possesses in himself a force, which gives him a power over others, and invests him with a responsibility towards Christ's little ones.

One may well shudder to think how much injury will be done to the moral well-being of a large number within the first few weeks of their residence here from forgetfulness of this charge; how many good principles may be undermined, how many noble resolves shaken, how many latent vices developed. I say nothing of the coarser forms of temptation. These wear no disguise, and therefore they condemn themselves. But reflect how much evil is inflicted from inconsiderateness, from levity, from insensibility to the effects of our commonest words and deeds. I will take one instance out of many which might be imagined. A man comes up here with certain religious views. He has been brought up, as we think, in a narrow school of theology. He pays undue regard to points which we consider non-essentials; he clings to certain religious watchwords with which we have no sympathy. Let it be granted for the moment that we are right and he is wrong. Yet his observance may be to him the sacrament of his highest moral duties; his watchword may be to him the embodiment of his truest spiritual convictions. Is it right, is it generous, is it kind, to laugh at his weakness, to pour scorn upon his scrupulousness? May not his error be better than our truth, his narrowness than our largeness of view? Is there no danger, lest while plucking up a prejudice, we may not root out a principle also? Men are apt to talk lightly of shocking prejudices, sometimes as if it were a matter of infinitely small moment, sometimes as if they were fulfilling an absolute duty, or at least acting an honest and upright part. What, if the veil were withdrawn, and they could see things as they are? What, if the cry of agony from Christ's little ones, whom they have wronged, should penetrate at length to their ears?

The subject is a wide one, and there is no time to pursue it further. Yet I cannot forbear saying a few words in reference to friendship. Friendship is the association of the stronger with the weaker. I do not say that the strength will be all on one side. Friendship in its very nature implies mutual dependence. Each has an element of power, which the other lacks; each therefore has a responsibility to the other, as to a little one in Christ. I do not forget (how could I ever forget?) that the friendships formed or cemented during residence here are valued as beyond all price by those who have known their blessings. I can hardly suppose that there is one man in this church to whom friendship is not a very sacred name. I cannot imagine any one here so base that he would not sooner cut off his right hand, than knowingly inflict a moral injury on his heart's best brother. But that which he would loathe to do intentionally he may do from carelessness. He feels his friend's strictness inconvenient to him; it interferes with the freedom of their intercourse; it leaves less time for amusement; at all events it acts as a barrier between them. It is an easy matter to weary or to laugh him out of it. And it seems a light matter too. But it may be terrible enough in its consequences. For it may be the first shock given to his moral nature; the first step taken on the downward incline. Or again, a man may be given to profane or idle talking. To himself it may mean little or nothing. But this is no measure of its significance to another. What glances off the surface harmlessly with him, may wound the soul of another deeply. And the wound festers, and spreads, and mortifies, and refuses to be healed. And thus from sheer recklessness he has sown the seeds of his friend's ruin. Can any agony be conceived more keen than the agony of a generous spirit, when the revelation is flashed in upon him, whether in this world or beyond the grave, of the cruel wrong he has done to one, whom he loved with more than a brother's love?

Against such perils as these I know only one security, the purification, the discipline, the consecration of the man's self. Be assured, if there is any taint of corruption within, it will spread contagion without. It is quite impossible to isolate the inward from the outward. No man can be always on his guard. 'Out of the abundance of the heart the mouth speaketh.' Each one of us carries about with him a moral atmosphere, which takes its character from his inmost self.

And this discipline, this purification of self, is best summed up in the Apostle's precept, 'In vice be ye children; howbeit in understanding be ye men.' The manly in the childlike, and the childlike in the manly —this is the true livery of the citizens of Christ's kingdom. Be men in the cultivation of your minds, in the vigour of your actions, in the courage of your lives, in the promptness to do and to suffer. But be children in frankness and simplicity; do nothing which you would care to conceal. Be children in natural affection; let home remain still the chief sanctuary of your heart. Be children in reverence; reverence is the body-armour of the young man's warfare. Be children, last of all, in faith and trustfulness; in all your trials and all your temptations, in your hopes and your fears, in your disappointments and your successes, in your weakness and your strength, seek repose in the embrace of the everlasting arms, confident of a Father's love. This do, and you will run no risk of offending Christ's little ones. This do, and the very God of peace will sanctify you wholly, that your spirit and soul and body may be preserved blameless unto the coming of our Lord Jesus Christ.

VIII.

FOLLY AND WEAKNESS TRIUMPHANT.

The foolishness of God is wiser than men; and the weakness of God is stronger than men.

1 CORINTHIANS i. 25.

Great S. Mary's Church, 20th Sunday after Trinity, 1876.

THE Apostle here represents the character and progress of the Gospel as a paradox. It is weakness superior to strength; it is folly triumphant over wisdom. It is an illustration—a unique and signal illustration—of God's mysterious working, whereby He chooses the base things of the world, yes, even the things that are not, to bring to nought the things that are.

This mode of working is not confined to revelation alone. History teems with examples of this paradox. For the most part the great crises in the progress of our race have been surprises of this kind. They have come from an unexpected quarter, or at an unexpected time. Their prime agents have not been the wise or mighty or noble in the estimation of the world. The reformer, or the avenger, has started up, as it were, suddenly from the earth beneath. It was an obscure Saxon monk, who broke up the empire of Papal ascendency, and created a new era in the history of intellectual and religious thought. It was an unknown Corsican adventurer, who dictated terms to a whole continent, made and unmade peoples and dynasties, and introduced as mighty a revolution in the world of politics as the other had done in the world of thought. There is perhaps a scarcely audible muttering of some social grievance; it is unheeded and unredressed; men go on their way, suspecting nothing; when suddenly the volcano bursts out under their very feet, and in a few short hours society is buried in fire and ashes. There is a silent stealthy idea, which insinuates itself into the crevices of human thought; it is hardly perceived, or, if perceived, it seems too insignificant to deserve attention; but it creeps and spreads, filling all the interstices, till the fabric, which has defied the storms of ages, cracked and loosened in every part, falls in ruins overhead. And then it is seen that God hath chosen the weak things of the world to confound the mighty.

But all illustrations of this Divine irony are faint and shadowy compared with the progress of the Gospel. Sacred history is an intensification of secular history. The triumph of the Cross is the paradox of all paradoxes.

No language is too strong for the expression of this fact in S. Paul's mind. These opening chapters of the Epistle are a very *Morias Encomion*, a Praise of folly and of fools. Does this account of his language seem extravagant? See how he describes the Gospel itself. His words are so strong, that we tacitly mistranslate or misinterpret them, in order to dilute their force. He speaks of the folly, the fatuity, of the thing preached, the Gospel message in itself ($\tau\hat{\eta}s\ \mu\omega\rho\acute{\iota}as\ \tau o\hat{v}\ \kappa\eta\rho\acute{v}\gamma\mu\alpha\tau os$). We render it 'the foolishness of preaching,' as if he were stigmatizing the weakness of the human, fallible advocate. He says that 'the foolishness,' or rather 'the foolish thing', 'of God is wiser than men.' We half unconsciously regard it as an *a fortiori* argument; as though he were maintaining that, if God's foolishness, God's lowest purposes, can so far transcend man's counsels, much more must God's wisdom, God's highest dispensations. But in fact he styles this very Gospel—this message of Christ crucified—a 'foolish thing' in itself. By what other name could he call it? It had been offered to the Greeks, the most cultivated, most intellectual, most keenly critical race of mankind, to the Greeks, who were the schoolmasters of the whole civilised world, and the Greeks had pronounced it unreservedly folly.

And not only is the message folly, but the messengers also are fools. So the Apostle describes himself afterwards. He is even proud of this strange distinction. 'We are fools,' he writes, 'fools for Christ's sake.' And again in the second Epistle, in a strain of lofty irony, he intreats his Corinthian converts, as they had always shewn a forbearing sympathy with men of feeble minds and senseless lives—notwithstanding the lofty intellectual eminence on which they themselves were placed—so now not to deny him this condescension which they had freely extended to others; 'As a fool receive me.' 'For ye suffer fools gladly, seeing ye yourselves are wise.'

And once more; if the messengers are fools, the recipients of the message must become fools also. It is necessary that the disciple should be in harmony with the teacher and with the lesson. He must sink all those pretensions which are his greatest pride. He must resign absolutely all claims to intellectual superiority or prudent discernment.

'Let no man deceive himself. If any man among you seemeth to be wise in this world, let him become a fool—that he may be wise.' Yes, none but a fool can appreciate this message of folly.

But this is not all. Folly itself may possess a certain brute force. The fool may be a giant in strength. What the brain lacks, the muscles and sinews may compensate. Does the Gospel possess any such advantage, as this figure implies? If it shews no wisdom, as the world counts wisdom, may it not possess some strength, as the world estimates strength? Nay, it is the weak thing of God, as well as the foolish thing—weak in itself, and weak in all its personal relations. Christ Himself, its theme, 'was crucified through weakness.' They, the preachers, are weak in Him. He, Paul, 'glories in infirmities;' 'takes pleasure in infirmities.' He declares himself 'glad,' yes, glad, that he is weak. Here again there is the same emphatic reiteration, as before. The Gospel is the very alliance of infirmity with folly. Its body is weakness; and its soul is foolishness.

Strange words these to address to a Corinthian audience. Corinth was a Roman colony on a Greek soil. As Greeks, his hearers set an excessive value on wisdom; and he recommends his message to them, because it is folly. As Romans, they worshipped power with an idolatrous worship; and he offers the Gospel for their allegiance, because it is weakness.

But stranger still than this encomium of folly, this panegyric of weakness, is the confidence with which he predicts its victory. The Apostle is quite sure that the folly of fools like himself will triumph over the wisdom of the wise. He does not shrink from declaring that the weakness of weaklings such as he is will dictate terms to the strength of the strong. 'God hath chosen the foolish things of the world to confound the wise; and God hath chosen the weak things of the world to confound the mighty.'

Could anything well have appeared more unreasonable, more reckless, more futile, than this confidence? Look at the two antagonists. Can you doubt for a moment to which side the victory must incline? At no other epoch in the history of the world would the Gospel have been confronted with a foe more formidable than at the actual crisis of its appearing. It found leagued against it all the wisdom of Greece and all the strength of Rome—a wisdom wiser, and a strength stronger, than mankind has ever seen before or after.

The human race has grown older in experience since then. Vast accumulations of thought and knowledge have been amassed. The collision of races and nations has from time to time struck out sparks, which have kindled the flame of the human intellect in some fresh quarter. But still the literature of Greece—its philosophy, its poetry, its oratory—enjoys a unique preeminence. It still supplies models for the imitation of a remote posterity. It is still fresh with the vigour of a perennial youth—a deathless power in the world of intellect and imagination. And yet these are only shattered fragments saved from the wreck of time, which we possess. What must it not have been then, when it was entire? What must it not have been then, when its language was still a living tongue—the medium of communication between all civilised peoples; when it was still upheld and interpreted by the religion, customs, institutions, daily life, of a race which had ramified and spread over every part of the known world?

And, as in the world of thought, so also in the world of action. In the whole life of the human race no power has arisen like the power of the Romans. There have been, and there are, empires which cover a larger superficial area. But for concentration, for unity, for available force, it has never had an equal. The greatest modern empires are rivals: each neutralises the power of the other. The domination of Rome owned no peer and no second.

The voice of Rome was the law of the world. It was the Roman's mission, said their great poet, 'to rule over the peoples, to spare the submissive, but to crush the proud and defiant.'

Confronted by this league of powerful allies, what was there in the story of Christ crucified that it should lead captive a reluctant world? We cannot, even with a conscious effort, realise all the repulsive associations which the Cross suggested to S. Paul's contemporaries. Substitute for the word some modern equivalent, as the gallows or the gibbet, and you approach more nearly to the idea conveyed. We shudder at such a substitution; we shrink from it as a profanation; our very reluctance shows how great a change has come upon mankind. Not in vain have eighteen Christian centuries passed over our heads. Not in vain has S. Paul's startling resolve—startling and repulsive when it was uttered, but obvious, self-evident, admirable now—to glory in nothing but the cross of Christ, been proclaimed from the pulpit Sunday after Sunday, and repeated day after day in thousands of Christian homes. Not in vain have saints been schooled to live, and martyrs nerved to die, in the strength of those words. The Cross is now the symbol of power, of heroism, of saintly patience, of triumphant love. But only reflect in what light it would be regarded by the Romans then? We ourselves, if we dwell on the repulsive aspects of the Cross, dwell chiefly, or solely, on the torture. But to the Roman the pain was only a small part of the horror. It was the ignominy of the punishment, from which he would turn away with disgust. No Roman citizen—however deep his crime—ran any risk of crucifixion. The law exempted him from this extreme degradation. It was the punishment of slaves, of the lowest and vilest of their kind. And they—these Romans, the masters of the world, with their proud bearing, with their innate respect for law, with their strong sense of political privilege —were invited by this Paul to fall down before a gibbet, and to admire a criminal condemned by a Roman magistrate to this most ignominious of all deaths. Weakness? It was far worse than weakness. It was vile, it was shameful—an outrage on all their most cherished feelings.

And, while thus repulsive to the Romans, this message of the Cross would be still less attractive to the Greek. With his gay spirit and his keen appreciation of the bright side of life, he could have nothing to say to this horrible tale of suffering. With his strong sense of beauty, he would avert his eyes with a shudder from this unlovely scene on Calvary. With his speculative cast of mind, with his eager craving after intellectual subtleties, how could he possibly find in this plain, this forbidding, this worse than common-place Jewish tale of an obscure convict, the answer to his philosophic questioning? It was folly, folly in its most foolish mood—this story of the Cross—to the Greek.

And, if it was such in itself, it would certainly gain nothing from the character of its advocate. S. Paul's opponents did not suffer him to indulge any feelings of self-complacency on this point. Their taunts served only to remind him that in his own person he illustrated the divine paradox. As was the Gospel, so was its preacher. Was he not weak? This was the very reproach which they hurled at him. They pointed to his insignificant stature; they glanced at his spare frame, worn out with toil and bowed down with sickness. He was a despicable object to these Corinthians, accustomed to the perfection of physical strength and grace in the athletes of their Isthmian games. They could not away with one who 'in bodily presence' was 'weak.' Was he not foolish also? Here again his enemies held up the mirror to him, and forced him to see his defects. This itinerant Jew, speaking with a foreign accent, breaking loose from all the approved forms of logic, defying all the established laws of rhetoric in his halting, tumultuous, solœcistic utterances—how could he hope to recommend his message to the fine ear and the fastidious taste of the Greek? Foolishness was not a strong enough word to express their estimate. He was 'in speech contemptible.'

Yes, he *was* weak, he *was* foolish. He could not gainsay the charge. Looking at his own heart, he condemned himself of foolishness far greater than that with which his enemies charged him. Reviewing his own life, he saw everywhere signs of weakness, which even their contempt had failed to detect. What were an insignificant presence and a faulty rhetoric after all, compared with the foolishness of a heart struggling against self, and the weakness of a life oppressed by the fears within and baffled by the fightings without? He *was* weak; he *was* foolish. Who knew this so well as himself? But what then? Strength was made perfect in weakness; wisdom started up full armed from the head of folly. Aye, there was a divine purpose in all this. He had this treasure, this priceless treasure in cheap, vulgar, fragile vessels of earthenware, 'that the excellency of the power might be of God, and not of himself.'

And so the cry of despair becomes the pæan of thanksgiving. The taunt of his enemies is the boast of the Apostle. He was not strong, but God's weakness was strong through him. He was not wise, but God's foolishness was wise in him. And this weakness, this folly, crushing all opposition, would press forward on its march from victory to victory.

A strange confidence to entertain. And yet this Paul was right after all. The centuries rolled on, and the prediction was fulfilled. The monstrous paradox, so contradictory to reason and so defiant of experience, proved true. All human calculation was baffled. The foolish things confounded the wise, and the weak things confounded the mighty. Neither the power and the polity of Rome, nor the philosophy and the arts of Greece, could check the triumphant progress of the Cross.

And do we ask how this triumph can be explained? S. Paul has answered the question by anticipation. 'The world by wisdom knew not God.' There is little danger that in this place you should underrate the intellectual and social triumphs of Greece and of Rome. Even as preparations for the Gospel, they hold a foremost place. What was the wisdom of Greece, but an elementary schooling for the higher spiritual lessons of Christianity? What was the power and organization of Rome, but the roadway of the Gospel of Christ and the scaffolding of the Church of God? But the arts of Greece and the polity of Rome had left a deep craving in mankind unappeased. Like the hart panting after the water-brooks, the soul of humanity was thirsting after a living God. It might not be altogether conscious of the object of its thirst; but the thirst itself was a terrible reality nevertheless. Men were feeling after God, but they had not grasped Him. He was near to every one of them, and they had not found Him. Wisdom had failed, and now it was the turn for foolishness.

Could he for a moment entertain any misgivings of its triumph? He knew what the Cross of Christ had been to himself. It had guided his zeal, it had purified his passions, it had widened his sympathies, it had opened his heart. It had filled him with new aspirations, new resolves, new hopes. That was no rhetorical figure, but a sober expression of fact, when he said that to be in Christ was to be a new creature, a new creation. In the light of this glory, all the lessons of the past had started up into new life: just as with the sunrise the landscape, which has appeared before a dark, indistinguishable mass, emerges in all the infinite beauties of form and colour. And, if it had been all this to him, a Hebrew of the Hebrews, what might it not be to these Gentiles tossed to and fro between the extremes of idolatry and scepticism? It was the touch of God, which mankind needed to heal the sores, to purge the corruption, to arrest the decay.

And he knew that this touch had thrilled through his inmost being in the revelation of Christ crucified.

'Man cannot live by bread alone.' This is the lesson which the triumph of the Cross teaches; a palimpsest traced in letters of fire on the erased page of an ancient civilisation; a voice emphasized by the thunder-crash of a fallen world. 'Man cannot live by bread alone'—whether the bread of social organization, of material appliances, of legislation, of polity (Rome had given enough and to spare of this); or the bread of intellectual culture, of æsthetic taste, of philosophy, of poetry, of art (Greece had dealt with these with a lavish hand). Fed to surfeiting with these, ancient society, nevertheless, had fallen from bad to worse, had become day by day more corrupt, more impotent, more helpless, till at length it lay seething in its own decay. And then the magnificent irony of God's purpose was seen. Foolishness triumphed over wisdom, and weakness set her foot on the neck of strength. And that which has been will be again, if ever the conditions should be repeated. If ever—I will not say science, but scientific speculation, should hold out promises which from its very nature it cannot perform; if ever, dazzled by its unparalleled triumphs, it should invade provinces which belong to another rule; if ever, consciously, or unconsciously, its representatives should attempt to eliminate from the Universe everything which renders possible either the guiding providence of God or the moral responsibility of man; if ever a materialistic philosophy should gain the ascendant, which offers no strength to the life struggling in the meshes of temptation, holds out no hand to the conscience staggering under the burden of sin, speaks no words of comfort to the soul torn with suffering or aching with bereavement; then, assuredly, soon or late the heart of humanity, finding itself deluded and betrayed, will rise in the name of conscience and faith, and turn upon its betrayer. Then again, as of old, the foolish things of the world will confound the wise. But then again, also, much that is useful, much that is beautiful, much that is true, may be buried in the ruin. The less must be sacrificed to the greater. Baffled, disappointed, starved in its highest moral and spiritual needs, humanity has no heart and no leisure for nice discrimination.

For this Cross of Christ—this strange, repulsive, foolish thing—did give to a hungry world just that food which alone could allay its pangs. Only reflect for a moment before we part, what ideas, what sanctions, what safeguards, what hopes, it has made the common property of mankind.

First of all: it went right home to the human

soul. It demanded no scientific training : it required no natural gifts. It addressed itself, not to the Greek as Greek, or to the Roman as Roman, but to the man as man. It took him, just as he was, stripped of all adventitious ornaments and advantages, and it spoke to his heart, spoke to his conscience, spoke from God to the godlike within him, but spoke nevertheless as a man speaketh with his friend.

And, so taking him, it set before him in the story of Christ's doings and sufferings an ideal of human life, absolutely pure, unselfish, beneficent, righteous, perfect, such as the world had never seen —an ideal, which once beheld could not be forgotten, but must haunt the memory of men for evermore, fascinating by its beauty, purifying, ennobling, transforming into its own bright image by the wonderful magic of its abiding presence.

And then again, it gave aid, where aid was most needed. It illumined the dark places of human existence. It dignified sorrow; it canonized suffering. The Cross of Calvary threw a glory over all the most harrowing and repulsive trials of life. Toil, sickness, pain, want, bereavement, neglect, obloquy, persecution, death—these were invested with a new meaning by the foolishness of the preaching. It was an honourable distinction now to share with Him—the head of the race—the prerogative of suffering. It was a comparatively light thing now to bear a little, where He had borne so much. Pain did not cease to be pain—whatever the Stoic might say; but pain had become endurable, for pain had been glorified.

And then again; it proclaimed in language, which could not be misunderstood, the universal brotherhood of man. The triumphs won on the Cross had obliterated, as in the sight of God, all distinction of race, of caste, of class. He the Crucified, He the Triumphant, was a poor artisan of a despised village of a despised nation—henceforth the accepted King of men, the Pattern of His race—the admired, honoured, worshipped of His brethren.

But above all, this Cross of Christ was the atonement, the reconciliation, of man to God. It united heaven and earth in an indissoluble union. It threw an unwonted and glorious light on the Fatherly mercy of God. It brought a new and unforeseen promise of pardon and peace, extended freely to all. Who shall despair now? Who shall dare to put limits to our Father's forgiveness? Who will refuse to Him the tribute of filial obedience? Who will not strive day and night to win His pardon, to win His favour, strong in the faith of this one perfect sacrifice —the supreme manifestation of Divine goodness and love?

These lessons, and others such as these, cluster round the Cross of Christ. And they can never fade or lose their freshness. What wonder then, if mankind preferred the folly of God to the wisdom of men? Here, and here only—in this old, foolish message of Christ crucified—is the promise and the potency of life, the one true and abiding life, the life that is now, and that shall be hereafter, eternal in the heavens.

IX.

BOUGHT WITH A PRICE.

Ye are bought with a price.
1 CORINTHIANS vi. 20.

Great S. Mary's Church, 1st Sunday in Lent, 1879[1].

THE words which I desire to consider with you this evening occur twice in the same Epistle. The connexion in the two passages is somewhat different; but the leading idea is the same in both. We have a Master, an Owner, Who has a paramount, absolute, inalienable property in us. We are His slaves, His chattels, His implements. All other rights over us are renounced, are absorbed, are annulled in His rights. He has acquired us by virtue of purchase.

---

[1] This was Bishop Lightfoot's farewell sermon, before leaving Cambridge for Durham. It was preached in the evening, and is not therefore strictly speaking a University Sermon.

In the first passage S. Paul is denouncing sins of the flesh. In his eyes these sins are something more than sins. They are flagrant anomalies; they are monstrous wrongs. There is a direct contradiction in terms, a flat denial of the first principles of justice, in the commission of them. God has set His stamp upon us. He impressed us with His image in our first creation. He re-stamped the same image upon us when He formed us anew in Christ. Thus we are doubly His. 'Here is God enthroned in the sanctuary of your bodies. But you—you ignore the august Presence, you profane the Eternal Majesty; you pollute, you dishonour, you defy, with shameless sacrilege, the ineffable glory, the Lord seated on His throne, high and lifted up, His train filling the whole temple of your being, as if He were some vile and worthless thing.' And then the Apostle suddenly changes his image: 'You are slaves—you are live chattels—nothing more. You have renounced all rights over yourselves. You are not your own; you were bought with a price. God in Christ is your Master. He demands your life, your soul, your all.'

In the second passage the Apostle is discussing a wholly different subject. He desires to set the existing arrangements of society in their proper relation to the Gospel. From this point of view the most perplexing problems were suggested by the deeply-rooted institution of slavery. What would come of this institution, when transplanted into the Church of Christ? How would the relations of master and slave be modified by this transference? The Apostle declines to discuss the matter in detail. Before the eternal verities of the Gospel, the conventional arrangements of society pale into insignificance. Freedom and slavery are endowed with a higher meaning. The slave is no more a slave, for he is set free in Christ. The free man is no more free, for he is enslaved to Christ. Yes, enslaved to Christ, because purchased by Christ. In outward matters the old forms of bondage to man may remain for a time, till they melt away before the broadening dawn of a higher principle. But the allegiance of the heart, of the soul, of the life, henceforth is due to no man, but to Christ alone. 'Ye were bought with a price; be not ye slaves to men.'

Not slaves to self, not slaves to men—this is the twofold lesson which we gather from the passages considered side by side. The ownership of self is done away. The lordship of our fellow-men is no more. One slavery alone remains, the most abject, most absolute, of all slaveries. We are the slaves of Christ.

The most abject slavery, and yet the most perfect freedom. This is the glorious paradox of the Gospel.

We are free, because we are slaves. We are most free then, when our slavery is most complete. Our servitude is itself our franchise. Our purchase-money is our ransom also.

I ask you all—I ask you young men especially—to lay this truth to heart to-night. Of all pitiable sights in this wide world I know none sadder than the spectacle of a young man drifting into an aimless, purposeless, soulless existence—soulless and purposeless, I mean, as regards any higher consideration than the mere wants and associations and interests of the moment, the mean routine of this mundane life. He does not stop to ask himself, Whence came I? Whither go I? Whose am I? Or, if he asks the question, he lacks the patience or the firmness to wait for an answer. And so he drifts—drifts into worldliness, drifts into unbelief, drifts into positive sin. Without a helm, without a compass, without sun or star in the heavens to guide him, he is swept onward whithersoever the tide of opinion, or the current of temptation, or the wind of circumstance may carry him, till at length he finds himself far away from the haven of God, and return is well-nigh hopeless. So he tosses about on the barren ocean for a while, and then he sinks into the abyss of darkness and despair. He has had no *ideal* in life.

Believe it, if you would rescue your lives—you and you—from this cruel shipwreck before it is too late, you must put the question definitely to yourselves, and you must be prepared to abide by the answer : 'What shall be the principle of my conduct? What shall be the goal of my life? What in short is my *ideal*, which shall animate, shall inspire, shall guide, my every act and my every word?'

Such an ideal is supplied you by the language of the text. It speaks of an absolute allegiance, a self-abandoning submission, an unswerving loyalty to One Who by an unquestioned title is your Lord and Master. It bids you find your truest freedom in your strictest servitude. It supplies you with a reason which is at once the seal of duty and the spring of affection. You were bought—bought at the heaviest price which God Himself might pay. You were purchased into servitude, but you were ransomed into liberty. You are no longer the slaves of self, because you are no longer the masters of self.

There is much foolish talk in these days about the relations of opinion to practice. It is not uncommonly assumed, even when it is not directly stated, that a man's beliefs are not of any particular moment, provided that his conduct is right. The underlying assumption is that beliefs exercise little or no influence on conduct. But does not all history, does not all human experience, give the lie to this assumption? Ideas have ever been the most potent engines in social and moral change. They have upset the thrones of kings, and they have reversed the destinies of nations. See what miracles have been wrought in our own time by the idea of national unity. Remember again what convulsions and upheavals of society were caused in the age of our fathers, and threaten again to be brought about in the age of our sons, by the idea of the equality and brotherhood of mankind. And as with nations and peoples, so also with the individual man. An ideal of life, firmly grasped, is an untold power for good or for evil. An ideal is a sort of prophecy, which works its own fulfilment; it haunts the dreams, and it inspires the waking hours. To keep a definite goal in view and to press ever forward towards it—to know what you desire to attain, and to strain every nerve for its attainment—this it is which will give a distinctness, a force, a savour to your conduct—a savour of life unto life, if the ideal be well chosen, but a savour of death unto death, if it be some unworthy aim, such as riches or ambition or pleasure or worldly success in any of its manifold forms.

The ideal, which the text presents to you, is the most potent of all ideals. Its potency consists in this, that it appeals, not only to our truest moral instincts, our aspirations after righteousness and holiness, but also to our deepest affections, our gratitude, our devotion, our filial love; and thus it grasps the whole man. The centre of this appeal is the Cross of Christ.

The Cross of Christ. To S. Paul Christ crucified was the lesson of all lessons; it gathered and absorbed into itself all other truths; it was the power and it was the wisdom of God. But we—we have stultified its wisdom, and we have enfeebled its power, by our too officious comments. Theologians and preachers have darkened, where they desired to make light. The simplicity of the Scriptures has been overlaid by technical terms; the metaphors of the Scriptures have been overstrained by subtle definitions. Redemption, atonement, imputation, satisfaction, vicarious punishment—what storms have not raged, and what clouds have not gathered, over these terms; till the very heavens have been shrouded in gloom, and where men looked for illumination, they have found only darkness over head and only confusion under foot. But ever and again to simple faith and to loving hearts the Cross of Christ has spoken with an awe and a pathos, which has taken them captive wholly. They were bought with a price. They cannot resist the appeal. They cannot deny the inference. They are no more their own.

'Bought with a price.' In these few words the lesson of the Cross is summed up. Whatever else it may be, it is the supreme manifestation of God's love. The greatness of the love is measured by the greatness of the price paid; and the greatness of the price paid defies all words and transcends all thought. When we try to realise it we are overwhelmed with the mystery, and we veil our faces in awe. We summon to our aid such human analogies as experience suggests or as history and fable record. The devotion of the friend risking his life to save another life as dear to him as his own—the bravery of the captain and the crew sinking calmly and resolutely into their watery grave, without a shudder, without a regret, disdaining to survive while one weak woman or one feeble child is left in peril—the heroism of the patriot hostage condemning himself to a certain and cruel death, rather than forfeit his honour on the one hand or consent to terms disastrous to his country's welfare on the other—all these have the highest value as examples of human courage and self-devotion. But how little after all does any such sacrifice help us to realise the magnitude of the Great Sacrifice. The analogy fails just there, where we look for its aid. It is the infinity of the price paid for our redemption, which is its essential characteristic. It is the fact that God gave not a life like our lives, not a weak, erring, sin-stricken, sorrow-laden victim like ourselves, but gave His only-begotten Son, gave His Eternal Word, to become flesh, to work and to suffer, to live and to die, for our sakes. It is the fact that the Glory of the Invisible God condescended to visit this earth; to hunger and thirst, to be despised, to be buffeted, to be racked and mangled on the Cross. The sacrifice is unique, because the Person is unique. Herein was love—not that we loved Him—did we not spurn Him, did we not hate Him, did we not defy Him?—but that He loved us. While we were yet sinners, while we were yet rebels and blasphemers, Christ died for us; and by that death God commends His love towards us—commends it, so that henceforth no shadow of doubt or misgiving can rest upon it.

Do we marvel any longer that S. Paul determined to know nothing among his converts but Christ crucified; that to him it embodied all the lessons, and concentrated all the sanctions, of the moral and spiritual life; that this weak and foolish thing stood out before his eyes as the very power and the very wisdom of God? In this one transcendent manifestation of God's purpose righteousness was vindicated, and love was assured, and ownership was sealed, and obedience was made absolute.

In the Cross of Christ righteousness was vindicated. At length sin appeared in all its heinousness. The greatness of the sacrifice was a mirror of the greatness of the sin. We are so constituted that we do not easily realise the magnitude of our wrongdoings, except by their consequences. I find that by my carelessness I have imperilled the life of another; and then my carelessness ceases to be a trivial fault. I am made conscious that by my selfishness I have deeply wounded the affections of another, and then my selfishness becomes hideous in my eyes. So it is here on a grander scale. Try to realise the significance of this death—its magnitude, its condescension, its goodness. And when you have realised it, go and sin, if you dare.

In the Cross of Christ love—God's love—was assured. When we look out into the world, we see not a little which perplexes and distresses. Sorrow and suffering, error, ignorance, anarchy, decay, death; these are the characters written across the face of nature. Men will not suffer us to slur over the legend of this handwriting, if we would. They point to the profusion of waste in nature, the many thousands of seeds that decay and perish for the one that germinates and blossoms and bears fruit. They bid us look at the pitiless cruelty of nature, creature preying upon creature, life sustained by the destruction of life, the whole face of the universe crimson with carnage. They bid us reflect on the many myriads of human beings who are born into this world and live and toil and die, without a joy, without a hope, without one ray of light from a higher world. And, having paraded before our eyes these trophies of imperfection, and worse than imperfection, they ask with a scornful triumph where is the providence of God, where is the Fatherly goodness on which we rely? Nay, we cannot deny the filial instincts which He has implanted in us, if we would. This is our answer to our gainsayers. But we—we have a further assurance in ourselves which silences all misgivings. The Cross of Christ rises as a glory before us, carrying the eye upward from earth to heaven, stretching right and left across the field of view, and embracing the universe in its arms. It tells of a love transcending all love. What room is there for doubt now? God is with us, and who then can be against us? 'He that spared not His own Son...shall He not with Him also freely give us all things?'

In the Cross of Christ ownership was confirmed. By all the ties of duty and of love we are henceforth His. No one else has a right to command us. Least of all have we a right to command ourselves. The purchase-money has been paid; and we are delivered over, bound hand and foot to do His pleasure. To hear some men talk, one would suppose that the

Cross was a clever expedient for securing the favour of God without requiring the obedience of man. They lay much stress on the one statement, 'Ye were bought with a price;' they altogether overlook the other, which is its practical corollary, 'Ye are not your own.' They forget that, if we were purchased into freedom, we were purchased into slavery also. And so by the violence of a spurious theology, faith and conduct, religion and morality, have been divorced; that which God joined together man has dared to put asunder; the moral sense has been outraged by the severance; and the Cross of Christ needlessly made a scandal to many. What, think you, would S. Paul have said to this interpretation of his doctrine—S. Paul, to whom faith in the Cross of Christ meant the recognition of His sole ownership, meant entire submission, obedience, slavery to Him, meant the subjection of every thought and word and deed to His will?

And so lastly; by the Cross of Christ obedience is made absolute. How can it be otherwise? Master this amazing lesson of Divine love, and you cannot resist the consequence. Your own love must be the response to His love; and with your love your unquestioning loyalty and submission. There is that in your very nature which obliges you to obey, if you will only listen. Once again, let us summon to our aid the poor and weak analogies of human love.

Have you never felt, or (if you have not felt) can you not imagine, the keen pain, which the sense of past ingratitude—unconscious at the time—will inflict, when long after it is brought home to the heart? A mother, we will say, has lavished on you all the wealth of her deep affection; you have accepted her solicitude as a matter of course; you have not been a disobedient son, as the world reckons disobedience; but you were wayward and thoughtless; you requited her attention with indifference; you almost resented her care at times, as if it were an undue interference with your freedom. And then death came. And some chance letter perhaps, found among her papers, revealed to you for the first time the riches of her love which you had slighted or spurned; and you are crushed with shame. No condemnation is too strong for your meanness, and no contrition is too deep for your remorse. Your ingratitude haunts you as a spectre, which you cannot lay. Death has robbed you of the power of making amends; and you are left alone with your baseness. And yet what is there in the tenderest mother's love comparable to the infinite love of Him Who became man for you, Who toiled and suffered and died for you?

This then is the ideal which the Gospel offers for acceptance to you young men to-day—this absolute subjection and loyalty to the Master Who bought you.

Welcome it now, before the inevitable years have pressed down the yoke of habit upon your necks. Welcome it now, while you can offer to Him the enthusiasm and the glory of a fresh and lifelong service. Do not think to put Him off to a more convenient season, purposing some time or other—you know not when and you know not how—to satisfy Him with the dregs of a wasted life. Each year, each month, will add pain to the effort. Lose your souls forthwith, that you may win them. Be slaves this very day, that you may be free.

Be slaves, and accept frankly the consequences of your slavery. To you, as to the chief Apostle of old, the mandate has gone forth, 'Follow thou Me.' Whither He may lead you, you cannot tell, and you must not too curiously enquire. It may be that in the years to come He has in reserve for you also some signal destiny, some work of unwonted responsibility, or some career of exceptional toil and pain, some cross or other, from which you would shrink with a shudder, if you could foresee it now. You are young yet. To-day and to-morrow you may gird yourselves, and walk whithersoever you will, roaming at large through the pleasant fields of life, and culling freely the joyful associations and interests of the passing hour. But the third day the grip of a Divine necessity will fasten upon you. Another will gird you and carry you whither you would not—far away from the home that you have cherished, from the friends that you have loved, from the work that has been a pleasure to you. Your ideal of life is shattered in a moment. Your hopes and projects for the future crumble into dust at the touch of God. Nay, do not repine. Follow Him cheerfully, whithersoever He may take you. Your cross will be your consolation; your trial will be your glory. The Lord is your shepherd; therefore shall you lack nothing. He shall lead you forth by the waters of comfort. Though you walk through the valley of the shadow of death, you will fear no evil; for He is with you; His rod and His staff shall comfort you.

To you more especially, the younger members of the University, my present and former pupils, my best and truest teachers, I would say a word in return for the many lessons which I have learnt from you. To one, for whom the old things of Academic life are now passing for ever away, the predominant thought must be the inestimable privilege which you and he alike have so bountifully enjoyed, and (it may be) so lightly esteemed. Believe it, you have opportunities here for the development of the higher life, which to many of you can never return again. In the ennobling memories and the invigorating studies of the place, in the large opportunities of privacy for meditation and prayer, in the counsel and support of generous and enthusiastic friendships, in the invaluable discipline of early morning Chapel, bracing body and soul alike for the work and the temptations of the day, in the frequent Communions recalling you in the spirit to the immediate presence of your Lord, in these and divers ways, you have a combination of advantages which no other time or condition of life will supply. Here, if anywhere, you may stamp the true ideal on your life. Here, if anywhere, you may rivet on your necks the yoke which is easy, and lift on your shoulders the burden which is light.

And to you, my older friends, my contemporaries, to whom I owe more than can ever be repaid, what shall I say? Forgive me, if I seem to be condemning you, when indeed I am only condemning myself. But now that the associations of this place are fast fading into a memory for me, I can only dwell with a sad regret on the great opportunities which it affords of influence for good—opportunities neglected at the time, only because they were not realised. How little would it have cost to overcome the indolence and shake off the reserve, to express the sympathy which was felt, to put in words the deeper thoughts which seethed in the heart but never rose to the lips! The value which younger men attach to such sympathy is altogether unsuspected at the time. The discovery comes too late—comes through the gratitude expressed for trifling inexpensive words and acts long since forgotten; and, when it comes, it overwhelms with shame.

But to young and old alike my word of farewell, if such it should be, from this pulpit is one and the same. Remember that you were bought with a price. Remember that henceforth you are not your own. Remember to be slaves now, that you may be free for evermore.

X.

BETHEL.

Surely the Lord is in this place; and I knew it not.
GENESIS xxviii. 16.

Great S. Mary's Church, 19th Sunday after Trinity, 1881.

AN unobtrusive, unimpressive scene, almost indistinguishable even to the curious eye of the archæologist 'in the maze of undistinguished hills which encompass it'—with nothing to attract the eye, and nothing to fire the imagination; large slabs of bare rock traversed by a well-worn thoroughfare; 'no *religio loci*, no awful shades, no lofty hills'—so is the site of Bethel described by the modern traveller. Yet this was none other than the House of God; this was the very gate of heaven.

An unimpressive scene in itself, but appearing still more commonplace, when contrasted with the famous shrines of heathendom—the rock fortress of

Athene, or the pleasant groves of Daphne, or the cloven peak of Parnassus, or the sea-girt sanctuary of Delos. No beauty, no grandeur, nothing of loveliness and nothing of awe, nothing exceptional of any kind, which can explain or justify its selection. Was there not ground for the wanderer's surprise on that memorable night? Why should this one spot be chosen to plant the foot of the ladder which connected heaven and earth? Why in this bleak wilderness? Why amidst these bare rocks? Why here of all places in the world? Yes, why here?

The paradox of Bethel is the paradox of the Gospel, is the paradox of God's spiritual dispensations at all times. The Incarnation itself was the supreme manifestation of this paradox. The building up of the Church was the proper sequel to the Incarnation.

Look at the accompaniments of the Incarnation. Could any environment of circumstances well have been imagined more incongruous, more alien to this unique event in human history, this supreme revelation of God's wisdom, and power, and beneficence? An obscure corner of the Roman world; an insignificant and down-trodden race, scorned and hated by the rest of mankind; an ox-stall for a nursery, and a carpenter's shop for a school—

what is wanting to complete the paradox? Yes, there is still one feature to be added to the picture —the crowning incongruity of all—the felon's death on the gibbet. Said not the prophet rightly, when he foretold that there should be nothing lovely in His life and circumstances, as men count loveliness; 'no form nor comeliness;' 'no beauty that we should desire Him'?

And the same paradox, which ruled the foundation of the Church, extended also to its building up. The great statesmen, the powerful captains, in the kingdom of God were fishermen and tentmakers. Never was this characteristic incongruity of the Gospel more signally manifested than in the preaching of S. Paul at Athens. Have we ever realised the force of that single word, with which the historian describes the impression left on the Apostle's mind by this far-famed city? Gazing on the most sublime and beautiful creations of Greek art, the master-pieces of Pheidias and Praxiteles, he has no eye for their beauty or their sublimity. He pierces through the veil of the material and transitory; and behind this semblance of grace and glory the true nature of things reveals itself. To him this chief centre of human culture and intelligence, this

Eye of Greece, mother of arts
And eloquence

appears only as κατείδωλος, overrun with idols, beset with phantoms which mislead, and vanities which corrupt. Art and culture are God's own gifts, legitimate embellishments of life, even of worship, which is the highest form of life. But if culture aims at displacing religion, if art seeks to dethrone God, why then in the highest interests of humanity be it our prayer that the sword of the barbarian and the axe of the iconoclast may descend once more, and sweep them ruthlessly away. There was, at least, this redeeming feature in ancient art, that it gave expression to whatsoever sense of the Divine lay buried in the heathen mind. But art and culture, which studiously ignore God—what can be said for these? In this one word κατείδωλος lies the germ of that fierce and protracted struggle of Christianity with Paganism, which ended indeed in a splendid victory, though not without inflicting many a wound on humanity of which the scars and seams still remain. Notwithstanding the merciless scoffs of a Celsus and the biting sarcasms of a Julian, the Apostle's words were verified in their literal truth. Strength was made perfect in weakness. God chose the foolish things of the world to confound the wise, aye, and the uncomely things of the world to confound the beautiful. The things which are not brought to nought the things which are.

So then in its accompaniments, not less than in its main idea, this incident at Bethel is a type of the Gospel of Christ. This exile, the representative of the Israel after the flesh, prefigures a greater outcast and wanderer, the representative of the Israel after the Spirit, the representative of the whole family of man. This ladder reared up from earth to heaven, whereby angels ascend and descend—what is it but the Incarnation of the Eternal Word, wherein God is made man, and man is taken up into God? This it is, which establishes the title of Christianity as the absolute and final religion of the world—this indissoluble union of the human with the Divine—this one only adequate response to the deepest religious cravings of mankind. Hence the Church has ever clung with a tenacity of grasp which shallow hearts could ill understand, to this central idea, the indefeasible wedlock of heaven and earth in the God-Man. And to those whose sight is purged by faith, to those who are gifted with the eye of the Spirit, the vision of Bethel will be vouchsafed with a far more exceeding glory; 'Verily, verily, I say unto you, Hereafter ye shall see heaven open, and the angels of God ascending and descending upon the Son of Man'—on the Son of Man; yes, and on thyself too, O man, for thou art one with this Son of Man, one with the Father in Him.

'Gifted with the eye of the Spirit,' I say: for in vain the heavens are riven asunder, and the glory streams forth, and all things are flooded with light, if the capacity of vision be absent. Only the cold bare stones beneath, only the midnight gloom overhead, only the dreary, monotonous waste around, these and these alone are visible otherwise. We have been saddened, perhaps we have been disconcerted, as recently we read the melancholy epitaph which sums up the creed of a brilliant man of science not long since deceased—a hopeless, soulless, lifeless creed, to which his own very faculties and acquisitions appear to us to give the lie. We have been saddened justly; but why should we be disconcerted? God be thanked, the most absolute childlike faith has not unfrequently been found united with the highest scientific intellect. We in this place have never yet lacked bright examples of such a union, and God grant we never may. But what right have we to expect it as a matter of course? What claim do the most brilliant mathematical faculties, or the keenest scholarly instincts, give to a man to speak with authority on the things of the Spirit? Are we not told on authority before which we bow, that a special faculty is needed for this special knowledge; that 'eye hath not seen and ear hath not heard;' that only the Spirit of God—the Spirit which He vouchsafes to His sons—knoweth the things of God? And does not all analogy enforce the truth of this lesson? One man has a keenly sensitive musical ear, but he is colour-blind. Another has a quick eye for the faintest gradations of colour, but he cannot distinguish one note of music from another. Does the imperfect eye of the one throw any haze of uncertainty over the hues of the rainbow; or the obtuse ear of the other disparage the master works of a Handel or a Mozart or a Beethoven? *Here* is a mathematician who sees in a sublime creation of imaginative genius only a tissue of unproven hypotheses; and *here* is a poet, to whom the plainest processes of algebra and the simplest problems in geometry are mere barbarian gabble, conveying no distinct impression to the brain, and leaving no intelligible idea on the mind. Judge no man in this matter. To his own master he stands or falls. But judge yourselves. Yes, spare no rigour and relax no vigilance, when the judge is the criminal also. Believe it, this spiritual faculty is an infinitely subtle and delicate mechanism. You cannot trifle with it, cannot roughly handle it, cannot neglect it and suffer it to rust from disuse, without infinite peril to yourselves. Nothing—not the highest intellectual gains—can compensate you for its injury or its loss. The private prayer mechanically repeated, then hurried over, then intermitted, and at last dropped; the devotional reading found to be daily more irksome, because suffered to be daily more listless; the valuable moral and spiritual discipline of the early morning chapel, gradually neglected; the unobtrusive opportunities of witnessing for Christ by deeds of kindliness and words of wisdom suffered to slip by—these, and such as these, are the unfailing indications of spiritual decline; till disuse is followed by paralysis, and paralysis ends in death; and you are left without God in the world. And yet when again—you young men—when again, in the years to come, can you hope that the conditions of your life will be as favourable to this spiritual self-discipline as they are now? Where else do you expect to find in the same degree the opportunities for private meditation and retirement, the daily common prayer and the frequent communions, the inspiring and sanctifying friendships, the wholesome occupation for the mind and the healthy recreations for the body, every appliance and every aid, which if you will only employ them aright, neither disusing them nor misusing them, will combine to build up and to perfect the man of God? Choose ye, this day. To you, more especially, I appeal who have recently commenced your residence here, and to whom therefore with the changed conditions of life a heightened ideal of life also is suggested. This is the momentous alternative. Shall your life hereafter be typified by the barren rocks and the monotonous waste, hard and dreary, if nothing worse; or shall it be illumined within and around with the effulgence of God's own presence, so that

> The earth and every common sight

to you shall seem

> Apparelled in celestial light,
> The glory and the freshness of a dream.

A dream? Nay, not a dream, but an everlasting reality, eternal, as God's own being is eternal.

There are two ways of looking on the relations between the things of this life and the things of eternity—a false and a true. The false way regards the one as the negation of the other. They are reciprocally exclusive. The avocations, the interests, the amusements of daily life—nature and history, poetry and art—these are so many hindrances to the heavenly life. Every moment given to work is a moment subtracted from prayer. Thus the inward life becomes a constant reluctation against the conditions of the outward. This is the spirit which of old peopled the desert with anchorites; the spirit which in all ages, though under divers forms, has made a religion of selfishness. This is the voice which cries, lo, here! and lo, there! though all the while the kingdom of heaven is within us, is in the very midst of us. The true conception is the reverse of all this. Its ideal is not a separation, but an identification of the two. It takes its stand on the old maxim *laborare est orare*. It strives that its work shall be prayer, and its prayer shall be work. Nature and history to it are not the veil of God's presence; they are the investiture of God's glory. And therefore to it is vouchsafed the vision of grace and comfort and strength, as to the patriarch of old. The solitary wanderer along the dreary thoroughfare of this life lays himself down. He has nothing but the bare stones beneath for a couch, and nothing but the midnight sky overhead for a tent. He closes his eyes for a moment; and the whole place is flooded with glory. Aye, the Lord was in this place, though he knew it not. He knew it not; but he knows it now—knows it in the access of strength, knows it in the promise of hope, knows it in the celestial voice and the ineffable light. All the common interests of life — the avocations, the amusements, the cares, the hopes, the friendships, the conflicts— all are invested with a dignity and an awe unsuspected before. Reverence is henceforth the ruling spirit of his life. This monotonous round of commonplace toils, and common-place pleasures, is none other than the House of God. This barren stony thoroughfare of life is the very portal of heaven.

To read these hieroglyphs traced on nature, on history, on the human soul—to decipher this handwriting of God wheresoever it appears, and where does it not appear?—is the ultimate and final study of man. All history is a parable of God's dealings; and we must learn the interpretation of the parable. All nature is a sacrament of God's being and attributes, and we must strive to pierce through the outward sign to the inward meaning. To realise God's presence, to hear God's voice, to see God's visage—let this be henceforth the aim and the discipline of our lives. So at length we shall pass from Bethel to Peniel—from the palace courts to the presence chamber itself. We shall see God face to face. It is a vision of power, of majesty, of awe unspeakable; but it is a vision also of purification, of light, of strength, of life. The blessing is won at length by that long lonely wrestling under the midnight sky. The fraud, the worldliness, the self-seeking is thrown off like a slough. All is changed. Old things have passed away. The supplanter rises from the struggle the supplanter no more, but the Israel, the Prince, who has power with God and with men. Shall not Moses' prayer then be our prayer, 'Lord, I beseech thee, shew me Thy Glory?'

'Shew me Thy glory.' Where else shall this glory reveal itself, if not in the studies of this place? These properties of numbers, these relations of space, these phenomena of light, of heat, of energy, of life, of language, of thought, what are they? Individual facts to be recorded, arranged, tabulated, marshalled under several heads, which we call laws and, having so called them, with a strange self-complacency and contentment fold our hands, as if nothing more were to be done, as if by the mere imposition of a name we had crowned them absolute sovereigns of the Universe? Or are they the manifestations—partial, indeed, and needing to be supplemented—of a power, a majesty, a wisdom, an order, a beneficence, a finality, a oneness, a One, Who is shewn to us as the Eternal Father in the revelation of the Eternal Son? Can we afford to look down from the serene heights of modern science and culture on the untutored Indian, who saw God's face in the shifting clouds, and heard God's voice in the whistling winds? Nay, was there not a truth in this childish ignorance, which threatens to elude the grasp of our manhood's wisdom? Was it altogether a baseless dream in those Stoic Pantheists, who endowed each several planet with an animating spirit of its own? Was it altogether a wild fancy in those Christian fathers which assigned to each its particular angel, who should whirl it through space and hold it in its course? Was it not rather a Divine instinct feeling after a higher truth? Human life cannot rest satisfied with the science of phenomena alone. It needs to supplement science with poetry. And the true, the absolute, the final poetry is the recognition of God the Creator and Governor, of God the all-wise and all-powerful, of God the Father, the Redeemer, the Sanctifier, of God the Eternal Love. Blessed are they who have eyes and see— they to whom

> The meanest flower that blows can give
> Thoughts that do often lie too deep for tears;

thoughts of immortality, of wisdom, of light, of love.

'Shew me Thy Glory.' Where else again shall His glory be seen, if not in those friendships which are the crowning gift of University life? This intimate communion of soul with soul, this linking of heart with heart, is it merely a matter of human convenience, of human preference, or has it a Divine side also? This love, this devotion, this reliance of the weak on the strong, this reverence for a nature purer, nobler, more upright, more manly, more unselfish than your own—what is its meaning? It is a precious, unspeakably precious, gift of God, you will say—far beyond wealth, or fame, or popularity, or ease, or any earthly boon of which you can conceive? Yes, but it is more than this. May we not call it in some sense a *sacrament*, a sign and a parable of your relation to your Lord? You are awed—no other word will express this feeling—you are awed with the honour done to you by this friendship. You do not talk much about it—it is too sacred a thing—but you do feel it. You confess to yourself day and night your own unworthiness. And yet, though you strive to be worthy, you would not wish to feel worthy. The very sense of undeservedness invests the gift with a bountifulness and a glory which you would not forego. The fountains of your thanksgiving would cease to flow freely, if you claimed it as a right; and it is a joyful and a pleasant thing to be thankful. Apply this experience to the infinitely higher gift of Christ's friendship, of Christ's sacrifice. Herein lies the power of the Cross—which men called, and still call, weakness—the power which awes, inspires, energizes, which elevates the heart and sanctifies the life—here in this feeling of boundless thanksgiving arising from this sense of absolute undeservedness. For is it not true, that those will love most, to whom most is given and forgiven? So then this your friendship is found to be none other than the House of God. The Lord is in this place, and happy, thrice happy are ye, if ye know it.

Once again; look into your own soul, and what do you find there? Yes, ye yourselves are the temple of the living God. He is there—there, whether you will or not. Through your reason, through your conscience, through your remorses and regrets, through your capacity of amendment, through your aspirations and ideals, He speaks to you. You are His coinage. His image and superscription are stamped upon you. Aye, and He has also re-stamped you, re-created you, in Christ Jesus by the earnest of His Spirit. If it be true of your body that it is fearfully and wonderfully made, is it not far more true of your soul? Henceforward you will regard yourself with awe and reverence, as a sanctuary of the Eternal Goodness. You will not, you dare not, profane this sanctuary. Here is the true self-respect—nay, not self-respect, for self is abased, self is overawed, self veils the face and falls prostrate in the presence of Infinite Wisdom and Purity and Love thus revealed. Surely, surely the Lord was in this place—in this poor, self-seeking, restless, rebellious soul of mine, and I thought it a common thing, I went on my way heedless, I followed my own devices and desires, I knew it not.

In conclusion, I have been asked to plead before you to-day a cause which it should not require any words of mine to enforce. The Barnwell and Chesterton Clergy Fund appeals to you year by year for aid. Of all claims this (I say it advisedly) should be a first charge on the liberality of members of the University. These populous and growing suburbs are created by your needs. They are chiefly peopled by college servants and others for whom you are responsible. Zealous clergy are willing to work for the work's sake in these districts commonly for stipends which no one could call remuneration—sometimes for no stipends at all. And yet it is still the same old story which I remember years ago. There is still the same difficulty in meeting current expenses; still the same fear lest the spiritual machinery should be impaired for lack of funds; still the same precarious hand-to-mouth existence, of which we heard complaint in years past. Is it quite creditable, that matters should go on thus? In a thousand ways you all, some directly, some indirectly, you all are reaping, materially, intellectually or spiritually, the fruits gathered from the liberality of past ages. Will you not make an adequate return? Steady, continuous subscriptions are needed. A liberal response to this day's appeal is needed. The Fund is largely dependent on the proceeds of the University Sermon. Not less than a hundred pounds will suffice to meet all requirements. Will you not give it this day, either in this church, or in contributions sent afterwards to the treasurer? Think not that you hear only the poor words of the preacher in this appeal. Christ Himself pleads with you. Christ's own words ring in your ears, 'Ye did it, ye did it not, to *Me*.' Ah yes, the Lord was in this place—in this weary pleading of the preacher, in these trite commonplaces of spiritual need; and *we*, we knew it not. God grant that you may know it in time. God forbid that He should ever say to you, 'I know you not.'

XI.

TRUE AMBITION.

I can do all things through Christ which strengtheneth me.
                                PHILIPPIANS iv. 13.

Great S. Mary's Church, 22nd Sunday after Trinity, 1883.

Πάντα ἰσχύω ἐν τῷ ἐνδυναμοῦντί με, 'I have strength for all things in Him that empowereth, enableth me.'

Ambition, the love of power, the thirst after influence—its use and its abuse, its true and its false aims—this is no unfit subject for consideration from a University pulpit.

Ambition in some form or other is an innate craving of man. All men desire power; they cannot help desiring it. The desire is as natural to them as the desire of health. Power and influence occupy the same place socially, that strength and vigour of limb do physically. Other desires, though veiled under various disguises, resolve themselves ultimately into a love of power. Knowledge is power. The cultivated intellect has a command of the resources of the universe. The selfish exaggeration of this feeling is a testimony to the underlying fact. The self-satisfied soul congratulates herself that she is

> Lord over nature, Lord of the visible earth,
> Lord of the senses five.

She communes with herself—

> All these are mine,
> And let the world have peace or wars
> 'Tis one to me.

Again, money is power. A man desires wealth, not for the sake of the stamped metal or the printed paper in themselves. These represent to him a command of resources. The miser indeed by base indulgence forgets the end in the means. In his own domain he resembles the spurious mathematician, to whom the letters and symbols are all in all, who sees in them so many counters and nothing more, who is blinded to the eternal relations of space and number which they represent. But traced back to its origin, the miser's love of money is a love of power.

Ambition, emulation, rivalry, plays a highly important part in the education of the world. We cannot shut our eyes to its splendid achievements. In politics, in social life, in mechanical inventions, in literature and art, its stimulus has produced invaluable results. If ambition has been the last infirmity, it has also been the initial inspiration, of many a noble mind. If by ambition angels fell, by ambition men have risen. It has heightened their ideal, and drawn them upwards from lower to higher. If it is chargeable with the worst evils which have devastated mankind, it must be credited also with the most splendid advances in human progress and civilisation.

Ambition has its proper home in a University. Ambition is the life of this place. What would Cambridge be without its honourable emulations, its generous rivalries? Body and mind alike feel the stimulus of its presence. Remove this stimulus, and the immediate consequence will be torpor and degeneration and decay. The athletic ambitions and the scholastic ambitions of the place, each in their own province, are indispensable to its health and vigour.

To one who, revisiting the scenes amidst which the best years of his life were spent, asks himself what topic may be fitly handled in this pulpit, the subject of ambition will naturally suggest itself. The University has lived through a period of exceptional restlessness and change during the last three decades —change far more considerable than during the preceding three centuries. Yet the spirit and life of the place are unchanging. It is the ceaseless, orderly march of a mighty army moving forward. Cross it where you will along the line, the gesture, the tread, the uniform, is the same; the faces only are different. It is the broad, silent, ever-flowing river, changeless, yet always changing. Wave succeeds wave; you gaze on it at intervals; not one drop of water remains the same; and yet the river is not another. The main currents of University life are the same now as thirty years ago. Its moral and social condition is mainly, we may say, the resultant of two divergent forces, its friendships and its emulations. It is the latter alone that I purpose considering this afternoon.

I speak to you, therefore, as to ambitious men. Those only are beyond hope who have no spirit of emulation, no craving after excellence—those only, in short, who are devoid of ambition. I invite you, therefore, to be ambitious. Only I ask you to purify your ambition, to consecrate it, to direct it through worthy channels and to worthy aims. I desire to shew you the more excellent way.

If indeed ambition has achieved splendid results, it can only have done so by virtue of splendid qualities. It must contain in itself true and abiding elements, which we cannot afford to neglect. Thus it involves a love of approbation. This cannot be culpable in itself. As social beings, we have sympathies and affections which lie at the very roots of our nature; and the desire of approval is inseparably intertwined with these. Who would blame the child for seeking to win its mother's good opinion? But the principle cannot be limited to this one example. It is co-extensive with the whole range of our social relations. The end sought is commendable. Only it may be discredited and condemned by the means taken to attain it; as, for instance, if we disguise our true sentiment, or withhold a just rebuke, or connive at wrong-doing, or sacrifice a noble purpose, for the sake of standing well with others. It is then, and then only, that the praise of men conflicts with the praise of God. Again, ambition implies a spirit of emulation. Neither is this wrong in itself. If it were, this University would stand condemned root and branch. Emulation is not envy; emulation is not jealousy; emulation does not seek to injure or rob another. An apostle avows it to be his aim to 'provoke to emulation.' This provocation—this stimulus of comparison and contrast—is an invaluable influence. We measure ourselves with others; we see our defects mirrored in their excellencies; our ideal is heightened by the comparison. Thus there gathers and ferments in us a *discontent* with ourselves—not indeed, if we are wise, with our capacities, not with our opportunities, not with the inevitable environments of our position, but with the conduct of that personality which is free to discipline, to mould, to direct, to develop our endowments. This dissatisfaction with self is the mainspring of all high enterprise and all moral advancement.

But the chief element in ambition is the pursuit of power. The consciousness of power gives a satisfaction quite independently of the exercise of power. Whatever form the power may take—whether intellectual eminence, or social influence, or physical strength, it is a thing which man desires, which he cannot help desiring, in and for itself. It is a seed of God's own planting—a germ of splendid achievements, if rightly trained and cultivated. It is only culpable in its excesses and aberrations. By our very constitution we feel a happiness in making the best of ourselves, as the phrase runs—in developing and improving our faculties, irrespective of any ulterior results. But a faculty improved is a power gained.

Brothers, I desire before all things to kindle in you a lofty ambition to-day. Therefore I have striven to justify ambition to you as God's very precious gift. I wish—God helping me—to inspire you with that inward dissatisfaction, that discontent with self, that ceaseless, sleepless craving after higher things, which gives you no rest day or night, because it pursues an ever-receding goal. I would stimulate in you that high spirit of emulation which, fermenting and seething in your hearts, impels you to unknown enterprises. I ask you to pray for power, to pursue power, to grasp at power, with all the force and determination which you can command.

How can I do otherwise? Are not you the men, and is not this the season, for the handling of such a topic?

Are not you the men? Who among you has not felt, at one time or another, the spark of a divine fire kindling within you? Who has not yearned with an intense, if momentary, yearning to do something worthy, to be something worthy? Youth is the hey-day of hope, of enthusiasm, of lofty aspiration. You have felt that there was within you a latent power, a heaven-born capacity, which ought to work miracles, if it were not clogged by self-indulgence, or cowed by timidity, or choked by sloth and indolence.

Are not you the men? As I have said to such audiences before, so I say to you now. You do not know, you cannot know, with what reverence—a reverence approaching to awe—older men regard the glorious potentiality of youth, in all the freshness of its vigorous life, with all the promise of the coming years.

Our habits are formed; our career is defined; our possibilities are limited. The wide sweep of moral victory, still open to you, is closed to us for ever. But what triumphs may you not achieve, if you are true to yourselves? What instruments may you not be in God's hands, if only you will yield yourselves to Him, not with a timid, passive, half-hearted acquiescence, but with the active concentration of all your powers of body and soul and spirit?

And again I ask, Is not this the time? The first volume of your life's history is closed. A clean page lies open, and with what writing shall it be filled? This is the great crisis of your life. These earliest few weeks of your University career, with which perhaps you are trifling, which you are idling thoughtlessly away, are only too likely to determine for you what you shall be in time and in eternity. It is the great crisis, but it is also the signal opportunity. Thank God, this is so; for the two do not always coincide. As the great break in your lives, it is the great season for revision, for repentance, for amendment, for the strong resolve and the definite plan. The old base associations must be abandoned; the old loose habits must be cured; the old indolence shaken off; and the old sin cast out and trampled under foot. Never again will such a magnificent opportunity be given you of rectifying the past; for never again can you reckon on the leisure, the privacy, the aids and environments, needed by one who is taking stock of his moral and spiritual life.

Who would not shrink from the responsibility of addressing you at such a crisis? And yet I speak boldly to you. Do I not know that, though the hand of the swordsman is feeble, yet the weapon itself is powerful—keener than any two-edged sword? Am I not assured that, though the preacher's words may be feeble, faltering, desultory, without force and without point, yet God may barb the ill-fledged, ill-aimed shaft, and drive it home to the heart? It is possible that even now the live coal from the altar may be brought by the winged seraph's hand, and laid on the sinful lips. I have undertaken to glorify the power of God, and to hold it up to you as your truest goal. How can I hope for a hearing, if I begin by distrusting it where I myself am concerned?

It is here, then, that I bid you seek and find the true aim of your ambition—in realising, appropriating, absorbing into yourselves, identifying yourselves with this power of God. It alone is inexhaustible in its resources, and infinite in its potency. There is no fear here lest the conqueror of a world should sigh and fret, because nothing remains beyond to conquer. If the craving is infinite, the satisfaction is infinite also. Star beyond star, world beyond world, will start out into view, as your vision grows clearer, spangling the moral heavens with their glories. πάντα ἰσχύω, 'I can do all things.' πάντα ὑμῶν, 'All things are yours.' Yes, but this promise of limitless strength has its condition attached, ἐν τῷ ἐνδυναμοῦντί με, 'In Him that empowereth me;' yes, but this pledge of universal dominion is qualified by the sequel, ὑμεῖς δὲ Χριστοῦ, 'Ye are Christ's.'

How can we better realise this power of God than by taking S. Paul's statement as our starting-point? The Cross of Christ is 'the power of God.' The Cross is the central revelation of God. The Cross has not unfrequently been preached as a narrow technicality, which shocks the conscience and freezes the heart. It thus becomes a mere forensic subtlety. But the Cross of Christ, taught in all its length and breadth and height and depth—the Cross of Christ, taught as S. Paul taught it—the Cross of Christ, starting from the Incarnation on the one side, and leading up to the Resurrection and Ascension on the other, contains all the elements of moral regeneration and of spiritual life.

(1) It is first of all *a lesson of righteousness*. It is the great rebuke of sin, the great assurance of judgment, the great call to repentance. Think—no, you cannot think; it defies all thinking—yet strive to

think, what is implied in the human birth, the human life, the human suffering, the human death, of the Eternal Word. Ask yourselves what condescension, what sacrifice, what humiliation, is involved in this. Summon to your aid all analogies of self-renunciation, which history records or imagination suggests. They will all fail you. No reiteration of the finite can compass the infinite. You are lost in wonder at the contemplation. And while your brain is reeling with the effort, try and imagine the awe, the majesty, the glory of a righteousness, which could only thus be vindicated. Then, after looking upward to God, look inward into your own heart, and see how heinous, how loathsome, how guilty your guilt must be, which has cost such a sacrifice as this. God's righteousness, your sin— these are brought face to face in the Cross of Christ.

(2) But, secondly, while it is a denunciation of sin, it is likewise *an assurance of pardon*. If the infinity of the sacrifice has taught you the majesty of God's righteousness, it teaches you no less the glory of His mercy. What may you not look for, what may you not hope for, from a Father, Who has vouchsafed to you this transcendent manifestation of His loving-kindness? 'He that spared not His own Son...how shall He not with Him also freely give us

all things?' Is any one here burdened with the consciousness of a shameful past? Does the memory of some ugly school-boy sin dog your path, haunting and paralysing you with its importunity? You feel sometimes as if your whole life were poisoned by that one cruel retrospect. Brother, be bold, and dare to look up. I would not have you think your sin one whit less heinous. But if God's righteousness is infinite, so also is His mercy. The Cross is reared before your eyes in this moral wilderness, where you are dying, where all are dying around you. Dare to look up. The bite of the serpent's fang is healed; the venom coursing through your veins is quelled; and health returns to the poisoned soul. Yes, and by God's grace it may happen that through your very fall you will rise to a higher life; that the thanksgiving for the sin forgiven will consecrate you with a fuller consecration; and that the acute moral agony, through which you have passed, will endow you with a more helpful, more sympathetic, more loving spirit, than if you had never fallen.

(3) But again; the Cross of Christ is not only a condemnation of sin, not only a pledge of forgiveness; it is likewise *an obligation of self-sacrifice.* 'God forbid,' says S. Paul, 'that I should glory, save in the cross of our Lord Jesus Christ.' But what next?

Not 'whereby I am saved in spite of myself,' not 'whereby I am spared all personal exertion,' but 'whereby the world is crucified unto me, and I unto the world.' This conformity to Christ's death, this crucifixion of self with Christ, always forms part of the doctrine of the Cross in S. Paul's teaching. The dying with Christ, the being buried with Christ, is the absolute accompaniment of the atoning death of Christ. We cannot be at one with Christ, unless we conform to Christ. The work done for us necessitates the work done by us. The potentiality of our salvation—of yours and mine—wrought through the Cross of Christ can only then become an actuality, when Christ's death is thus appropriated, realised, translated into action by us—by you and by me. But it remains still the work of God's grace. Human merit is absolutely excluded still, as absolutely as by the baldest and most unqualified doctrine of substitution.

(4) Fourthly and lastly; the Cross of Christ is *a lesson of the regenerate and sanctified life.* Dying and living, burial and resurrection, these in the Christian vocabulary are correlative ideas. The Crucifixion implies the Resurrection and the Ascension. The raising up on the cross demands the raising up from the grave, the raising up into heaven. The lifting up of the brazen serpent in the wilderness is the symbol

alike of the one and the other. And as with Christ, so also with those who are Christ's. 'If we died with Christ, we shall also live with Him.' Those only can be made conformable to Christ's resurrection, who have been made conformable to His death. The power of His resurrection is the counterpart to the power of His cross.

Herein then—in the Cross of Christ—resides this power of God, which is offered to you as the true aim of your ambition, inexhaustible, omnipotent, infinite. Will you close with the offer? Then reverence yourselves; believe in yourselves; consecrate yourselves.

Reverence yourselves. Begin with reverencing this your body. Reverence it as God's handiwork fearfully and wonderfully made. Contemplate it; yes, contemplate it with awe, if only for its marvellously subtle mechanism. But reverence it still more as the consecrated temple of God's Spirit. Do not neglect it; do not misuse it; before all things do not defile and desecrate it. Young men, the problem of social purity is thrown down for your generation to solve. Will you accept this challenge? The conscience of England is awakening to the terrible curse. To redress the crying social wrong, to raise womanhood from degradation and shame, to hold up to reverence the ideal of a pure, chivalrous, manly manhood—this is the crusade in which you are invited to enlist. Will you, as consecrated soldiers of the Cross, claim your part in the glory of this campaign? If so, the work must begin now, must begin in yourselves. There can be no success against the foe, where there is disaffection and mutiny in the citadel.

Believe in yourselves; yet, not in yourselves as yourselves. Believe not in your strength, but in your weakness. Believe in God Who dwells in you. Give full rein to your ambition. Trust this power of God. It will not stunt nor mar, will not crush, will not annihilate your natural gifts—your social endowments, your political instincts, your intellectual capacities. It will only elevate, harmonize, inspire, purify them. Trust this power. There is nothing, absolutely nothing, which you may not do, if you will only trust it. πάντα ἰσχύω, 'I have strength for everything,' everything in heaven and earth. You have youth, health, vigour, enthusiasm, hopefulness, everything on your side now. Seize the great opportunity which can never return.

Consecrate yourselves. Empty yourselves of yourselves, that you may be filled with God. Yield yourselves to Him, not with a passive acquiescence, a sentimental quietism, but with the earnest, energetic direction of all your faculties to this one end. A period must still intervene for most of you before the active independent work of life begins, a period of discipline and waiting. Only by patience will you win your souls. But the self-dedication must be made at once, and it must be complete. Half-heartedness spoils the sacrifice. Postponement is perilous. The opportunity despised turns its back on you for ever. Consecrate, consecrate yourselves, body and soul and spirit, to God now, this night.

I have been asked to plead before you a cause of the highest moment to the welfare of this town. I shall dismiss it very briefly. I will not do you the dishonour of supposing that long and earnest pleading is needed from me. You have brought together large populations in the outlying suburbs to minister to your wants, to your convenience, to your pleasure— alas, in some instances to suffer shame and wrong from your recklessness. The provision for their spiritual wants is therefore a first charge on your temporal wealth. This fund, for which I plead to-day, is in many cases the only instrument, in all the chief instrument, in providing for these wants. But its finance is always precarious, unless on these occasions we raise about a hundred pounds. For a hundred pounds therefore I ask. Let those who have not brought ample gifts, send them afterwards, that there be no shortcoming.

But there is another matter also, which I desire to lay before you. Eleven years ago an effort was made to build a church at New Chesterton, a rapidly growing suburb, inhabited largely by college servants. The preacher from this pulpit then appealed to the undergraduates. He asked if there were not among the younger of his hearers twenty-five men who would offer themselves as collectors among their companions. Not twenty-five, but thirty-two, offered themselves in answer to this appeal. A very considerable sum was collected by these means from undergraduates. With the contributions gathered in this and other ways the Church of S. Luke was erected, an incomplete structure to be finished hereafter. The parish work has gone on vigorously ever since. The clergy give their services for very inadequate remuneration, or no remuneration at all. There is daily service, morning and evening. The church is full on Sunday mornings, crowded to overflowing on Sunday evenings. The communicants have increased manifold; the offertories are large for a poor parish. The spiritual ministrations are thus cramped for want of room, and the completion of the structure is a pressing need. Has not the time arrived for another such appeal to the undergraduates? Are there not five-and-twenty, are there not fifty young men now, who would undertake a like charge? I cannot suppose that undergraduate zeal has waned in these eleven years. Everything that I see and hear leads me to take a far more hopeful view. In Christ's name and for Christ's sake come forward and offer yourselves for this work.

www.ingramcontent.com/pod-product-compliance
Lightning Source LLC
Chambersburg PA
CBHW030317240426
43673CB00040B/1193